To My

NEW YORK TIMES BEST SELLING AUTHOR

Friends Marty & Nancy

THIS IS NOT
YOUR FATHER'S
DEMOCRATIC
PARTY

with Best wishes and love —

WILLIAM SYLVESTER NOONAN

First Copy!

ISBN: 1477600957
ISBN-13: 9781477600955

DEDICATION

For My Father
Thomas Joseph Noonan

In honor of the centenary of his birth in the
pivotal political year of 1912

Requiescat In Pacem

Table of Contents

PREFACE

This effort is a personal observation by the author via his father's life experiences and affiliation with the Democratic National Committee. It is written with hope that it appeals to readers who also long for "their" father's Democratic Party to return to its core principles of fairness, support of the middle class, and to bring people of all walks of life together for healthy and productive debate. The storyline becomes a personal reflection when the author reaches voting age in the bicentennial celebration year of the "Spirit of '76".

INTRODUCTION

It is a Tuesday evening in mid-January 2010. Nothing is really happening as it is the coldest and bleakest time of the year in Boston. My children are upstairs doing their homework; my wife is in the kitchen, cleaning up after dinner. Like every other suburban male in Massachusetts, I am clicking away on the television remote control, looking for something to entertain me for the balance of the evening.

A local news alert catches my eye. The reporter, broadcasting live from an election-night hotel reception, bears remarkable news. It appears that the dark horse Republican candidate is leading the special election for the US Senate seat recently vacated by the death of Teddy Kennedy.

I can't believe what I am hearing. A Republican winning any election in Massachusetts is noteworthy, but a Democrat losing the Liberal Lion's seat after nearly half a century is more than just good copy—it is historic.

Outside his district, Republican State Senator Scott Brown is virtually unknown to the citizens of Massachusetts. About six weeks prior, he won his party's primary for the chance at the US

Senate seat. An exercise in futility. So what? The Republicans always throw the latest "up-and-comer" into the general election, but GOP nominee is always swatted away by the Democrats and dismissed by the press.

This is Massachusetts after all. It's Kennedy's seat, and any Democrat—whoever won the primary—would be our next US senator. It is a foregone conclusion. Even Vegas wouldn't make book.

Maybe it was the new decade or maybe it was Barack Obama's first year as president that gave Massachusetts voters sticker shock, but one thing was for sure. They had endured the cold weather and broke the boredom of January to send their message: It was time for a change. From the reporter's point of view, this revolutionary act in Massachusetts would be known as the "Scott heard 'round the world."

The Democratic candidate was Massachusetts Attorney General Martha Coakley. She was bright, liberal, sturdy, untarnished, malleable, and a woman—the perfect Democratic candidate for the Senate. Once she had won the primary, national Democrats arrived with financial assistance and political guidance. The party engaged a number of Kennedy-connected, national special interest groups to raise funds on Coakley's behalf.

Unfortunately, this quickly led to an erosion of her credibility. When a Weekly Standard reporter went to Washington to cover a health care lobbyist group's fund-raiser for Coakley, he was thrown to ground by security right in front of her for reasking a challenging question about her statement that there are "no terrorists in Afghanistan."

The instincts of the Massachusetts voters took over. How could our leading legal authority apathetically watch as an esteemed journalist is physically assaulted and his First Amendment rights are trampled right in front of her and not have the mettle to defend him or chastise her bodyguard? Instead, she referred to the reporter as a Republican "stalker" and sashayed away.

This, along with Coakley's unprecedented litany of media gaffes, set the stage for a political upset. Forget about the "no terrorists in Afghanistan" statement—we could live with that idiocy. But when questioned on a local radio show about Boston Red Sox pitcher Curt Schilling, who was supporting Brown, her response was that he was a "Yankees fan." A collective groan could be heard from Beantown to the Berkshires.

Did she not remember that in Massachusetts, as favorite son Tip O'Neill had famously noted, "All politics is local"? She did not know her local Red Sox lore? Had she slept through the fascinating 2004 playoff series against the Yankees that set the stage for our first World Series championship in eighty-six years? To the legendarily sports-crazed commonwealth, this was blasphemy. She never recovered.

Her vulnerability was now so obvious to the populace that the Democratic Party ramped up its support. There were acts of desperation from Washington. The president came to town. Bill Clinton came to town. Since when do leading national Democrats need to come to Boston to provide political endorsement?

As Election Day grew closer, Obama and other left-leaning luminaries reached out to us with "robocall" messages pleading for a Democratic vote. Obama's health care bill was before Congress, and without Teddy's presence or influence, every vote counted.

On the other side of the aisle, Scott Brown had been building a grassroots base for months, and it was paying off handsomely. The contrasts between Brown and our two most recent senators were both humorous and obvious.

Brown stole a page out of Senator John Kerry's presidential playbook by wearing his barn jacket when campaigning. When the commonwealth's junior senator campaigned against George W. Bush, "the worst president ever," in 2004, he traveled the country in a barn jacket that appeared to be either brand new or recently dry-cleaned. The image was clearly contrived and shallow as a birdbath. No one bought his baloney that wearing a barn jacket made him a regular guy, because he is not. Everyone knows he is an Ivy League elitist, married to inherited Republican wealth.

Scott Brown actually owned and wore a barn jacket on a daily basis—and usually when driving his famous pickup truck. He was an authentic, regular guy, not one who played one on television to win elections. Additionally, since the Chappaquiddick incident, no one in Massachusetts had seen Teddy Kennedy driving anything but his yacht, and to Teddy a "pickup" was a blonde, not a truck.

The contrasts with Kerry and Kennedy did not stop there. Brown was local, a standout high school athlete, not a prestigious prep school alumnus. He was not wealthy or married to wealth. He was hardworking and smart, putting himself through college and law school. He was handsome, a former male model, married to a local news anchor with two young, attractive daughters, all of whom actually lived in Massachusetts. He was committed to public service as an officer in the Massachusetts National Guard, and unlike Kerry, cameramen did not film him when he was on maneuvers.

Scott Brown was a breath of fresh air, and he was one of our own, a true native son. All of this resonated with Massachusetts voters, and they were going his way and away from an old way of doing business.

Astonished that I was witnessing history, I began to cheer him on. I don't know why. It was like an out-of-body experience. My wife appeared.

"What's going on?" she inquired.

"Scott Brown is beating Martha Coakley!" I exuberantly replied.

"Well, I voted for him. We talked about it. Didn't you?" she inquired, nonplussed.

"Yeah, but only to send a message. I never thought he could pull it off," was my response.

My puzzled wife looked at me and asked, "And you're cheering him on? I can't believe it, you of all people. What would your father say?"

She had a point. I was very familiar with this Senate seat and its past four occupants. My father helped John F. Kennedy wrest it away from the Republicans in 1952 and defend it with a historic plurality in 1958 to ensure that he had the momentum to run for president in 1960. I knew the guy who kept the seat warm for Kennedy's little brother, Teddy, to become old enough to run for the seat. I knew Teddy Kennedy well. I knew his family, stayed at his house, and worked on his campaigns. I consider the man the governor appointed to the seat after Kennedy's death a family friend. And here I am cheering the Republican on. What had happened to me? Had I become a cynical contrarian, an apostate? What was happening to Massachusetts, to the Democratic Party, to the nation? This was Armageddon to someone like me, yet I was digging it.

I admit I have voted for Republican presidential candidates in the past, but never for any other national office. No matter how much I disagreed or disliked the Democratic candidate, to cast a vote for a Republican in Massachusetts was sacrilege, a waste of time. One hundred percent of the commonwealth's representatives in Washington are Democrats.

Most of the mayors, the majority of selectmen, the city council members, and State House officials are Democrats. Sure, there might be a few Republicans peppered here and there, but for the most part, if you hold an elected position in Massachusetts, you are probably a Democrat. The sun rises in the east, sets in the west, and Massachusetts sends Democrats to Washington; drunks, homosexuals, pedophiles, Catholic priests, and even felons have been elected to Washington every two years by Massachusetts voters. That is just the way it goes.

In 1972, Massachusetts was the only state in the nation to vote against the Nixon reelection landslide. Since Watergate and Nixon's resignation, we wore this distinction like a badge of honor and we gloated in our "We told you so" pomp. Yup, we were the bleeding hearts—left-leaning, dyed-in-the-wool liberal Democrats.

But now things had changed, almost overnight. With the death of Teddy Kennedy, the halls of Massachusetts politics were quiet in the absence of his booming voice, his corny jokes, his sentimental songs. He was, we had now learned, irreplaceable.

The cold winds of change blew through Massachusetts's political alleyways and back streets that night. Old yellowed newspapers with historic Democratic headlines irrelevantly swirled in the ignobility of the frigid January air.

How had this happened? When did Democratic candidates become professional politicians and not policy makers? What happened to the intellectual elite, the noblesse oblige, the best and the brightest? Where were Wilson's New World Order, Roosevelt's New Deal, JFK's New Frontier, and LBJ's Great Society? Had the party gone too far left?

Was it Bill Clinton's expedient political rhetoric and ambition rather than firm national policy that changed the party? Was it Gore's childish antics? Maybe it was Obama's hollow message of "Hope and Change" that shoved the Massachusetts populace outside the Democratic tent and into the cold and uncertain air.

I knew that tent well. It was modern and fashionable when I was a boy. I watched its fabric get ripped and repaired only to become stronger and more durable; against the Dixiecrats, against the hawks, even in spite of anarchists and assassins.

I can recall the leaders inside that tent—professors, scholars, diplomats, activists, union officials, and hardworking people. I remember proud and patriotic veterans, as well as glamorous women smoking extralong cigarettes and sipping daiquiris. I remember fresh-faced Ivy League school kids, ready to change the world, feed the hungry, house the homeless, heal the sick, educate the ignorant, end war, promote peace, and bestow civil rights. Where are they now?

Recently, to me, that tent seemed exploited, dirty, dishonest, and diseased. Somehow these Ivy League kids had evolved into political snake oil salesmen. Madison Avenue-marketed candidates who lacked the intelligence to empathize and the integrity to compromise in order to promote policy. Now they have no real agenda, except to placate the lobbyists, raise money, and get reelected. Who was going to save the party from these interlopers?

Candidates now say and do whatever they need to be elected. They hurl divisive and judgmental accusations at their opponents. Clinton wagged his finger at us, blaming the press, of all estates, and his right-wing opponents for the Lewinsky conspiracy, all the while lying and deceiving the nation, even under oath.

The Democratic baby boomers eroded the nation's trust in elections, quarreling over "hanging chads" like spoiled children, thinking more of themselves than collective nationalism. Even Nixon, after losing to Kennedy in 1960, the closest of all presidential elections, fraught with accusations of voter fraud and tampering, dismissed the possibility of a recount to preserve the common good and his public image. Not Al Gore. He took his whiny battle all the way to the Supreme Court, taking the sanctity of that institution and the voting process to the cleaners, instead of taking it like a man.

Yet in spite of impeachment, adultery, resignation, and utter bullshit, amazingly the press, like an abused yet faithful wife, stood by the side of the Democrats. How many times has this scene been re-created since Bill Clinton? By Eliot Spitzer, by John Edwards, by Jim McGreevey, and Anthony Weiner. Granted, it is not just Democrats who cheat on their wives, but these judgmental and sanctimonious individuals are the ones who scream the loudest at their opposition.

Now, standing outside the tent, looking in, I remembered what Ronald Reagan had said: "I didn't leave the Democratic party. The party left me."

Recently, I had been feeling the same way, and this night was evidence that I was not alone. I determined that the Democratic Party I had joined as an eighteen-year-old, my father's party, like his Oldsmobile did not exist anymore. It was irrelevant and forgotten, rusting away in some old junkyard. Where did it go, and what was I going to do about it? How could I answer these questions? Similar to psychoanalysis, I needed to go back in time to find the true spirit of my party and locate at what divergence did it cleave itself from reality and lead us to this abysmal pool of mediocrity.

Courtesy of the Woodrow Wilson Presidential Library, Staunton, Virginia

1

WOODROW WILSON & WORLD WAR I

The year 1912 was momentous. The Republic of China was established, the African National Congress was founded, Native American Jim Thorpe won gold medals at the Olympic Summer Games in Stockholm, the Marines landed in Cuba, the United States occupied Nicaragua, the First Balkan War began, the *Titanic* sank, vitamins were discovered, Universal Pictures was incorporated, the Oreo cookie was introduced, the Boston Red Sox defeated the New York Giants in the World Series at newly christened Fenway Park, my father was born to a couple of young Irish immigrants, and Woodrow Wilson was elected the twenty-eighth president of the United States.

Wilson was the first Democrat elected president in over thirty years and only the second since before the Civil War. It had been quite a run for the Republicans, so the 1912 election remains the historical turning point for the "progressive" policies of the twentieth-century Democratic Party.

As a matter of historical reference, the origins of the Democratic Party were established by Thomas Jefferson in 1790s as an opposition party to his political adversary, Federalist John Adams. Although once allies during the deliberation and drafting of the US Constitution, the two men grew to be political opponents.

Adams was a plump and pompous attorney from Massachusetts who favored a strong central government and a globally respected financial epicenter in the Northeast. Jefferson, on the contrary, was a strapping intellectual southern farmer from Virginia who advocated a small central government, individual states' rights, constitutional self-reliance, and autonomy from the influence of the New York banking families.

Jefferson dislodged Adams as president after one term to become our third president. Affectionately known as the "people's president," Jefferson purchased the Louisiana Territory from France, tripling the acreage of the nation, and sent the Lewis and Clark Expedition into the wilderness to map what he had acquired. He also signed a bill into law prohibiting the import of slaves into the United States. This historical period is known as Jeffersonian Democracy and the First Political System.

When the Federalist's son, John Quincy Adams, sought the presidency in 1824, General Andrew Jackson, "Old Hickory", the hero of the Battle of New Orleans, now a Democratic senator from Tennessee, opposed the younger Adams. It was an incredibly contentious election, and although Jackson won the popular vote, he failed to attain the required electoral votes. Under the rules of the Twelfth Amendment, the outcome of the general election was to be determined by the House of Representatives. A corrupt bargain between Speaker of the House Henry Clay and Adams swayed the election in Adams's favor. Adams subsequently appointed Clay secretary of state.

Jackson resigned his Senate seat and, with his cohorts, refashioned the Democratic Party to include a coalition of obscure and defunct political organizations from the previous century. When a political cartoonist lampooned Jackson as a "jackass", the donkey became the symbol of the Democratic Party. Jackson's combined forces handily defeated Adams's reelection in 1828.

Jackson, like Jefferson, was a southerner and a classic liberal. He so disliked the Northeast banking families, claiming they ignored farmers, southern farmers in particular, that he abolished the Second Bank of the United States by rescinding its federal charter, withdrew government funds, and paid off the entire national debt. While short-lived, it is the only time the nation has ever been debt free. This political period in American history is known as Jacksonian Democracy and the Second Party System. Today the Jefferson-Jackson Day dinner remains the highlight of the Democratic National Committee's annual fundraising calendar.

The actual Democratic National Committee was not established until 1848. The first presidential nominee, Lewis Cass, was defeated by General Zachary Taylor of the powerful Whig Party. The issue of slavery had become the Democratic Party's political albatross. To Democrats, slavery was a moral issue. To the South, it was a pure economic necessity.

Any hope of cooperation between the two parties was dashed when a Democratic Congress passed the Compromise of 1850, which dealt with slavery concerns in the territorial spoils of the Mexican-American War. It was an unholy alliance, and the results were bittersweet at best. Although the Compromise did destroy the once powerful Whig Party, allowing Democrats to win the next two presidential elections, it also brought the nation to the brink of civil war.

During and after the Civil War, Democrats remained the opposition party until the back-and-forth elections of Grover Cleveland in the 1880s. Cleveland was elected, then rejected, and then reelected, making him the only man in US history to serve nonconsecutive presidential terms. During this period of American history, the country was pretty much run by Republican presidents from Ohio.

During the 1896 presidential campaign, the loquacious Democrat William Jennings Bryant (depicted as the Cowardly

Lion in the *Wizard of Oz*: all roar and no courage) challenged Republican William McKinley (presumably the Wizard) on the theoretical concept of Progressivism. The concept became popular, especially among southern farmers, but Jennings lost the election. Four years later Bryant took on McKinley, again with no luck. On this Republican ticket, McKinley chose New York Governor Theodore Roosevelt as his running mate.

At forty-two years of age, Roosevelt was a highly accomplished man. A wealthy Knickerbocker from Manhattan, Roosevelt graduated Phi Beta Kappa from Harvard. After graduation, he authored a well-respected naval history analysis of the War of 1812. For his efforts he was appointed assistant secretary of the navy. He relinquished the post only to join the cavalry during the Spanish-American War, leading the charge up San Juan Hill to win a decisive battle. As a returning war hero, Roosevelt was quickly elected governor of New York and two years later joined the incumbent ticket as McKinley's vice presidential candidate, as the previous vice president Garret Hobart, had died in office.

Six months after his inauguration, McKinley was assassinated by an anarchist in Buffalo, New York and Vice President Theodore Roosevelt became the nation's youngest president. In spite of being a Republican, Roosevelt was also a Progressive.

The Progressives were a collection of highly educated elitists who sought to purify and reform government by reengineering the plebeian dynamics of how politics as usual was conducted. By exposing political corruption at the parochial ward boss level and at the national Tammany Hall level, the Progressives hoped to establish a more modern and sensible approach to how government was managed, especially within the social parameters of economics, education, medicine, industry, and religion.

Roosevelt bowed to President Washington's protocol of serving just two terms in office and handed the presidential reigns over to his good friend and Cabinet member William Howard Taft. The fifty-year-old Roosevelt retired to read, write, and hunt large game, or so he thought.

Upon his return from an African safari, Roosevelt found his nation in disarray. Taft had spilt the Republican Party by personally and legally offending the very industries Roosevelt had spent eight years cultivating. As Roosevelt publicly chastised Taft, an irreparable rift divided the once-great friends and political allies.

At the 1912 Republican National Convention in Chicago, Roosevelt attempted to wrest the presidential nomination away from Taft, but at the last moment, he was outmaneuvered. Undeterred, Roosevelt started a third party, the Progressive Party, and challenged Taft in the general election. Roosevelt defeated Taft, but in doing so, spilt the Republican Party, allowing political newcomer, Democratic New Jersey Governor Woodrow Wilson, to waltz into office.

Thomas Woodrow Wilson, the son of a Presbyterian minister, although southern-born, is best remembered as a northern "modern liberal" intellectual. Wilson was a highly educated man, possessing a PhD; he served as president of Princeton University before entering politics. In 1910, he was elected governor of New Jersey during the anti-Taft hysteria that also gave Congress back to the Democrats. Two years later, Wilson was a candidate for the highest office in the land.

During the summer months of the 1912 presidential election campaign, Governor Wilson lunched with Progressive attorney Louis D. Brandeis, one of the nation's leading legal thinkers and a future Supreme Court justice. Brandeis enlightened Wilson to the Progressive's philosophy of ending industrial monopolies by eliminating special interest groups and establishing government regulation that encouraged competition and protected the ordinary worker. Wilson embraced Brandeis's theories and implemented them into his campaign rhetoric under the banner of "The New Freedom."

When Wilson assumed the presidency in March 1913, the country was a paradox of socially and economically disadvantaged rural farmers and newly minted, culturally refined, urban industrialists. Due to economic realities, rural farmers became laborers in the industrialists' factories. As the framers of the Constitution envisioned only an agrarian United States, the industrial revolution remained unregulated by the government. As such, there were countless strikes and disputes between labor and management. Wilson sought to bring the old world and the new world together in the spirit of equality and mutual respect.

"No one but the presidency seems to expect...to look out for the general interests of the country," he stated.

Supported by a Democratic House and Senate, Wilson got busy. He did not wait for legislators to come to see him; he went to Capitol Hill. Utilizing the little-known "President's Room" in the Capitol as his office, Wilson frenetically cobbled together progressive domestic legislation. He called for a joint session of Congress and delivered a State of the Union, the first president to do so since John Adams in 1799. Wilson became known as the first modern-day president.

His first act of progressive policy was the Underwood-Simmons Tariff Act. Throughout the 1800s the federal government imposed onerous duties on European products in an attempt to protect struggling homespun American manufacturers. As industrialized America began to prosper, the tariffs had become antiquated and burdensome. By lowering the European tariffs, Wilson effectively leveled the international playing field for both the consumer and the American manufacturer. Furthermore, Wilson offset the missing revenue of European tariffs with the newly ratified Sixteenth Amendment, authorizing a federal income tax. It was a win-win scenario.

Wilson's next order of business was the Federal Reserve Act. He again called for a joint session of Congress and proposed a unified banking and currency system for nation. In 1913 there were over seven thousand unregulated banks nationwide, each issuing its own form of currency. By establishing a central banking system and granting it authority to issue legal tender, Wilson created the most ethical and respected banking system in the world.

Like Jefferson and Jackson before him, Wilson did not trust the wealthy New York banking families or slick Wall Street financiers. In order to keep the Federal Reserve Banks from being centralized in the Northeast, Wilson geographically divided the nation into twelve regional districts. The act was both political genius and economically prudent, as neither Washington nor New York were offended.

Next, Wilson established the Federal Trade Commission to promote competition while protecting the consumer from unfair business practices. He followed with the Clayton Antitrust Act. Called the "Magna Carta of Labor" by Samuel Gompers, the act ended union liability antitrust laws and established proper protocol for labor unions' rights. The act also promoted ethical business guidelines that held management personally responsible for violations. So began the love relationship between unions and Democrats.

Having accomplished legislation to keep industry ethical and competitive, Wilson now sought to assist the nation's farmers. He employed agricultural agents to educate uninformed farmers of new scientific farming techniques and postindustrial-age farming equipment. He established the Federal Farm Loan Act to assist farmers with long-term, low-cost mortgages, protecting them from foreclosure.

In the aftermath of the *Titanic* tragedy, Wilson ordered all ships to be retrofitted with new safety equipment and the proper amount of lifeboats. Under the Seamen's Act of 1915, he sought guidelines and protection for the Merchant Marines who were being attacked by German U-boats. He lobbied for women's voting rights. He passed child labor laws. He did it all.

"Can't you let anything alone?" Wilson was asked.

"I let everything alone that you can show me is not itself moving in the wrong direction, but I am not going to let those things alone that I see going down hill," he replied.

His efforts and accomplishments were unparalleled. In his first two years in office, he achieved more legislative victories than any president before or since.

"It was not the Democratic Party, but God, who made me president," he once proclaimed.

Yet he did have his foibles; bending to congressional pressure, Wilson reversed a prior edict and ordered the segregation of Negroes at US Civil Service programs. He also had no voice in the passage of the Nineteenth Amendment, prohibiting the sale of alcohol.

With all of his domestic successes, Wilson had many international issues to address. The world was in chaos. Most notably, there was a war raging in Europe. In the northern Atlantic Ocean, German U-boats attacked civilian passenger ships with Americans civilians on board.

"America is too proud to fight" was his platform, as if confrontation were philosophically beneath him.

Wilson was reelected in 1916 under the motto "He kept us out of war," but his reelection victory was by the slightest margin, and the reality of international turmoil was about to be unleashed.

His first term had been marred by many international incidents; Mexico was his greatest source of aggravation. Even though Mexico was an unstable nation with many violent internal revolutions, when Arizona and New Mexico were granted statehood in 1912, Mexican nationalists invaded the United States, claiming the new states were Mexican territories.

Wilson did not want to go to war with Mexico, but he was unwilling to be pushed around. After a series of diplomatic snubs, border skirmishes, and the false arrest and incarceration of US Marines, Wilson finally attacked Mexico, with mixed results.

In his second term, a diplomatic telegraph between Germany and Mexico was intercepted by the British and shared with the United States. Essentially the Germans were seeking an alliance with Mexico to invade the United States. Wilson viewed the telegram as an act of war and took his position to Congress.

"The war to end war" was his battle cry. In his delivery, he stressed his objective of entering and winning the war and to make "the world safe for Democracy." So, with congressional approval, the United States was at war with Germany.

Wilson started the Selective Service System, known as the "draft," and conscripted over 2.8 million men into military service. By the summer of 1918, the United States was sending ten thousand troops to Europe each day. The Germans had underestimated our immediate response and rapidly found themselves losing ground. With over six million battlefield causalities, no military reserves, and the German economy devastated, the Kaiser halfheartedly surrendered on November 11, 1918, Armistice Day, now known as Veterans Day.

The Treaty of Versailles, the official end the "Great War," was not signed until spring 1919 in Paris. Wilson attended the signing, using his progressive Fourteen Points policy as the blueprint for his concept of the League of Nations, the precursor of the United Nations. Wilson, like Progressive President Theodore Roosevelt before him, was awarded the Nobel Peace Prize for his efforts.

Wilson might have effectively lobbied the League of Nations to his European counterparts, but his political adversaries at home, especially Senator Henry Cabot Lodge, would wear him down. While campaigning in Colorado for its approval in Congress, Wilson collapsed from a stroke, leaving him physically incapacitated. Woodrow Wilson served the balance of his term as an invalid, hidden away within the White House, the United States never joined his League of Nations.

Wilson died in 1924, long before his insight of an institution of international cooperation, now known as the United Nations, would come to fruition. Wilson's faith in institutions, particularly ones that promoted peace, military deterrence, and international conflict resolution, is his lasting epitaph.

Subsequent Democratic administrations have used Wilson's innovative policies as the cornerstone to tirelessly fight to defend and protect the common man from exploitive capitalists, cold-hearted bankers, and unethical financiers. They have also fought for the rights of the worker, the farmer, the widows, and orphans.

Since Wilson, who considered himself as the first leader of the free world, Democratic presidents have fought and won a second world war, engaged in two full-scale anticommunist wars, provided assistance in numerous minor conflicts, and survived the Cold War. They have enacted massive domestic legislation for the civil rights of minorities, the aged, the sick, the unemployed, and the uninvited.

In the century since Wilson's election in 1912, the year of my father's birth, the face of Democratic Party has evolved from a stoic, bespectacled, lily-white WASP from the world of academia seeking "social justice," to a cool, hip, dark skinned "community organizer" from a small Pacific island, seeking "socialism."

Let us explore the Democratic Party's ideological evolution from Wilson's progressive reforms to the contemporary ideology of Barack Obama and determine what, if any, the two Democrats have in common, a century later.

2

HAPPY HOUR & HERBERT HOOVER

By the time of the 1920 presidential election, my Irish immigrant grandfather had put down his shovel and secured a job as a ticket taker on the Boston & Maine Railroad. Apparently he was quite the charmer with his uniform and hat, his brogue, and his gold watch fob, announcing the arrival and departure times of the nation's most advanced form of transportation.

Yet the country had grown weary of the Democrats. Warren G. Harding ran as the Republican candidate under the banner "Return to Normalcy," implying that Wilson's legislative accomplishments, the Great War, and the Paris Peace Treaties were too much for the nation to ingest in eight years.

The nation agreed and returned to its historical predilection of hiring Ohio Republicans to the highest office in the land. Harding won by a landslide and became the first sitting United States senator to be elected president.

The Harding administration was a disaster. As the rest of the nation was observing Prohibition laws, President Harding and his "Ohio Gang" were gambling and guzzling illegal whiskey in the White House. When questioned by the press, his response was essentially; as president, he could do whatever the hell he wanted inside the Executive Mansion. This arrogance, along with rumors of infidelity, an isolationist policy, and numerous political scandals, marks him as one of the nation's worst presidents. He died in office, just eighteen months into his administration. Even in death there were rumors that his wife had poisoned him.

Vice President Calvin Coolidge assumed the office at Harding's death. Coolidge, a taciturn New England Yankee, the former governor of Massachusetts, made famous by his stance on the 1919 Boston Police Strike, was a polarizing personality compared with Harding. "Silent Cal," as he was known, took a laissez-faire attitude to business and considered the Republican landslide of 1920 an indictment of Wilson's aggrandizing international posturing. Coolidge was reelected in 1924; it was the Roaring Twenties, after all.

The financial prosperity of the 1920s brought us Herbert Hoover, the secretary of commerce during the Harding-Coolidge administrations. He beat Democrat Governor Al Smith in a 1928 landslide.

Hoover was a political neophyte who had never held elected office. He was, however, a highly confident and prosperous man. An orphan at ten years of age, he matriculated to the first graduating class of Stanford University with an engineering degree. Later he made millions of dollars in international mining. Stationed in London after the end of the Great War, he personally organized the relief efforts that fed the starving Europeans, especially the people of Belgium. He was revered for his phenomenal success in business and as an international humanitarian, and he was promptly recruited into the public sector.

Coolidge abhorred the man, stating, "He has been giving me advice these last six years, all of it bad." Yet, Coolidge, learning from Teddy Roosevelt's Progressive Party blunder of 1912, did not want to split the Republican Party again, so he blessed Hoover's successful campaign.

The stock market crash of 1929 set in motion an economic downturn that led the nation into the Great Depression. During a six-year run during the Roaring Twenties, the Dow Jones Industrial Average (the Dow) had increased five-fold, peaking at 381.17 in September 1929. It teetered there for a few weeks until the last week of October, when it began to sell off. In a period of three days, the Dow lost over 30 percent of its value. The Dow finally hit bottom in July 1932 at its record low of 41.22, losing nearly 90 percent of its value in three years. It did not return to its previous peak for twenty-five years.

There were many economic factors that led to the Great Depression, but it happened on Hoover's watch, and he got the blame. Hoover sought self-reliance and local volunteerism rather than governmental intervention to solve the economic disaster. Out of despair, he increased the federal tax brackets from 25 percent to 63 percent, never a good idea in a depression.

It was too late for my grandfather. After loosing his job on the B&M railroad during the Depression, he suffered a near-fatal heart attack and was now unfit for work. For an Irishman who left the auld sod for a new life and opportunity in America, being idle was unbearable.

My father was away at college on scholarship. He was called home in the fall of his freshman year to provide for his mother and multiple siblings. He was barely twenty years old but now the head of the household.

Being an accomplished high school athlete, it was not hard for him to find a job working at the municipal athletic facilities in Brookline, Massachusetts. He secured a job as a lifeguard at the "Tank" America's first public indoor swimming facility. Later he parlayed that into a coaching position and played semipro baseball in his spare time. A local baseball booster took an interest in his pitching ability and sponsored a local team. My uncles told me that hundreds of people would show up to watch these games for two reasons: These were baseball's glory days as America's favorite pastime, and the games were free.

My grandfather, the rascal, discovered the health benefits of a recreational romp and added a couple of more kids to his brood. I can only imagine the discussions my grandmother and father were having at the kitchen table. She had her last child when my father was twenty-six years old. My father was so busy he never noticed she was pregnant. When he asked how all this happened without his knowledge, he was told, "'Tis no man's business." Typical Irish.

My father was having a hard time making ends meet, and he took a part-time job driving a supply truck for the baseball benefactor, which led to him learning his first business model. When the benefactor unexpectedly died, his widow did not know what to do with the business and asked my father for advice. After a quick meeting with a wealthy associate, my father was the proud owner of a medical bookstore across the street from Tufts Medical Center in Boston. In spite of Hoover, whom he disliked, he was pursuing his right to happiness and achieving the American dream.

Sadly, his favorite sister, born on his eighteenth birthday and his Goddaughter, died one day of a ruptured appendix. Seems a doctor could not get to the house in time to diagnose the condition, and the poison invaded her body. She was three years old, and he never spoke of her again. Years later, he gave her name to his only daughter. One day I found the little girl's Mass card, bearing my sister's name, in his daily missal, and I asked him about it. He got up and walked out of the room. My mother explained to me that it drove him crazy that all that his sister needed was proper medical attention to stay alive. I was told never to broach the subject with him again. I never did. Those were tough days in America.

For his sins, Hoover was drummed out of office by New York Governor Franklin Delano Roosevelt (FDR) in a landslide victory in 1932. From one landslide to another. Hoover is now considered by many experts as one of the worst presidents in the nation's history. Although he was extremely capable before and after his presidency, the Great Depression will forever tarnish his sterling reputation.

3

ALPHABET SOUP
& SOCIAL SECURITY

Courtesy of the Franklin D. Roosevelt Presidential Library

Franklin Roosevelt was a proud and ardent admirer of distant cousin Teddy, even wearing the outdated pince-nez eyeglasses to mimic his appearance. Franklin married Teddy's favorite niece, Eleanor, whom Teddy gave away at the altar. The two Roosevelt presidents shared much in common besides their surname—both were Harvard educated and held similar governmental appointments and elected offices—but Franklin was a Democrat.

In those days there was a four-month interregnum between Election Day and Inauguration Day. During this time the nation continued to stumble and falter. Banks failed, unemployment soared to fifteen million, or nearly 25 percent of the population, and bread lines grew longer. Hoover attempted to lure the president-elect into a meeting to discuss the possibility of a joint effort to halt the economic downturn, but FDR would not take the bait. Knowing it was a political maneuver, Roosevelt sat quietly and waited for his administration to begin on March 4, 1933. The day before he took the oath of office, more than five thousand banks failed. His inaugural address was heroic and set the stage for the greatest financial recovery, ever.

"This is preeminently the time to speak the truth, the whole truth, frankly and boldly. Nor need we shrink from honestly facing conditions in our country today. This great nation will endure as it has endured, will revive and will prosper. So, first of all, let me assert my firm belief that the only thing we have to fear is fear itself"

FDR immediately began a one hundred-day bloodless revolution that would become known as the "New Deal." On his first day as president, Roosevelt declared a four-day bank holiday and closed every bank in the country.

On March 9th Congress passed, and FDR signed the Emergency Banking Relief Act, which gave Treasury officials the right to inspect a bank's ledgers. If the bank was fiscally sound, it was allowed to reopen. The president was also given the power to control credit, currency, and foreign exchange. In time public confidence in banks was restored.

Less than two weeks later, Roosevelt cut federal employee payrolls by 15 percent. A few days after that, he authorized 3.2 percent beer and wine sales to increase tax revenues, in spite of the Nineteenth Amendment prohibiting the sale of such libations.

On March 31st, he founded the Civilian Conservation Corps (CCC), which hired over 250,000 unemployed men between the ages of eighteen and twenty-five. The CCC was a peacetime army that built and rebuilt the nation's infrastructure and revitalized the nation's natural resources.

Roosevelt created the Tennessee Valley Authority (TVA), which enabled the federal government to build dams and power plants to bring energy and industrial development to the area. He established the Emergency Transportation Act to increase regulation of the nation's railroads.

He took the nation off the gold standard, and although economists decried the move as the end of Western civilization, Roosevelt was praised by the House of Morgan for saving the country from "complete collapse." As the stock market began to rise, foreign trade increased, consumer prices rose, and economic confidence returned.

On June 16th, his hundredth day in office, Roosevelt introduced three major New Deal reforms. The Glass-Steagall Act secured bank deposits with the Federal Deposit Insurance Corporation (FDIC) and separated commercial banks from investment houses. The Farm Credit Administration saved farmers from foreclosure and refinanced their mortgages. Roosevelt also subsidized their products and used the surplus to feed hungry Americans. For the average American, he reissued mortgages at more reasonable interest rates and lent them money to pay back taxes and finance home repairs. Lastly he established the National Industrial Recovery Act (NRA), which expanded Wilson's fair practices policies and guaranteed labor's rights to organize and bargain collectively. The act also created the Public Works Administration (PWA) to provide construction jobs for the unemployed.

Part of his New Deal legislation was the Securities Act of 1933, which regulated the offers and sales of securities (i.e., stocks and bonds) to potential investors. This was a good-faith measure in response to the unregulated abuses by investment firms that led to the 1929 stock market crash, the catalyst of the Great Depression.

In all, sixteen major pieces of legislation were passed in his first one hundred days in office. Roosevelt publicly thanked Congress for assisting him in his quest. A real class act, as promised, he delivered "a leadership which aims at a larger good."

These were heady days indeed. It had been twenty years since Wilson had crafted so much progressive legislation. Seldom does one see immediate results in new legislation, but in the case of FDR, consumer confidence in the banks began to recover, and when the banks begin to recover, the sun started to shine again and people began singing "Happy days are here again," still the proud anthem of the Democratic National Committee.

Roosevelt's hands-on approach, his bold actions, and sunny disposition restored public faith in the nation. The fact that he peddled his ambitious policies to the press each week earned him great respect from the Fourth Estate, members of which never once mentioned the fact he was paralyzed by polio and confined to a wheelchair. Yet it was his patrician eloquence and down-home manner during his radio "fireside chats" broadcasts from the White House that restored the nation's confidence. Life in America may not have been all warm and fuzzy, but Roosevelt had stopped the hemorrhaging and survived the operation. Only continued hard work and glowing optimism would heal the nation's ills.

Some of the industries he saved were critical of his actions, but Roosevelt was undeterred. The New Deal pushed for more regulation of commodities, investments, and banking. FDR expanded national labor regulations, interstate commerce rules, and employment projects. He imposed a "wealth tax," which aroused the rancor of his fellow millionaires, but it was the creation of the Social Security Administration that really infuriated them.

The only way that Roosevelt could get Congress to approve the Social Security Act of 1935 was to make it available to everyone. It was an extension of his Good Neighbor Policy. Funded by payroll taxes on employers and employees, Social Security provided a system of old age and supplementary retirement payments. It also provided assistance to widows and orphans and medical assistance for the impaired. Historian Arthur Schlesinger Jr. noted, "The federal government was at last charged with the obligation to provide its citizens a measure of protection from the hazards and vicissitudes of life."[1]

FDR believed that since he was elected president by the entire nation, he was hired to serve as the chief executive of the land. It was he who governed the nation, he who diagnosed its ills, and he who prescribed the elixir to the people's elected representative in Congress. From there it was up to Congress to determine which agency was to administer his programs and to how to fund them. By embracing centrist legislators from both parties, he was able to forge the greatest legislative agenda since Wilson and right the nation's economy.

FDR also enjoyed being a Democrat. As a realist, he demanded party allegiance and put an end to accusatory finger-pointing by congressional Democrats, who had remained in a minority status since Wilson. Although he admitted that the presidency was "a terrible job, but someone has to do it," he also seemed to enjoy being president. Most evenings he held

---

1 Arthur M. Schlesinger Jr., The Coming of the New Deal, Boston and New York: A Marnier Book, 1958, p. 315.

a cocktail hour in the White House, shaking up martinis and demanding that no politics or policies were to be discussed.

"For the sympathy, help, and confidence with which Americans have sustained me in my task, I am grateful. For their loyalty I salute the members of our great party, in and out of political life in every part of the Union. I salute those of other parties, especially those in the Congress of the United States who on so many occasions have put partisanship aside... We have conquered fear."[2]

It was no surprise that FDR won his reelection in 1936 with another landslide. He also elevated the Democrats back to a majority standing: 331 to 89 in the House of Representatives and 76 to 16 in the Senate. It is said by Democrats, to be the greatest election of all times.

Despite his resounding reelection mandate, Roosevelt's second term would be bogged down by pettiness and politics. In his second inaugural address, he stated, "I still see one-third of a nation ill housed, ill clad and ill nourished...I assume the solemn obligation of leading the American people forward along the road over which they have chosen to advance."

When the Supreme Court unanimously declared the National Industrial Recovery Act unconstitutional, Roosevelt went ballistic, calling the justices "nine old men." Without

---

2 FDR-Democratic National Convention Acceptance Speech for Renomination, 6/27/1936.

even consulting congressional Democrats, he sent a proposal to Capitol Hill to expand the Supreme Court to fifteen justices and authorize the executive branch the ability to appoint one new justice for each who refused to retire by age seventy. Although the proposal failed to win approval by the Senate Judiciary Committee, the Supreme Court slowed its obstruction of additional New Deal policies.

Roosevelt's programs may have righted the American ship of state, but they had little benefit for the rest of the world. The tentacles of America's Great Depression had encircled the globe.

By rightfully being so preoccupied with our own economic issues, the United States had unwittingly become an isolationist nation. In Europe and Asia a terrible Axis of Evil had formed an unholy alliance that would soon define not only the remainder of Franklin Roosevelt's presidency, but also the remainder of the twentieth century.

4

THE WACKOS OF WORLD WAR II

In reality the United States had never been a global force in international relations or foreign affairs until the beginning of the twentieth century. After a litany of minor Caribbean revolts, the Monroe doctrine, the War of 1812, and constant skirmishes with Mexico, the United States was still very much a territorial power in the mid-twentieth century.

From the spoils from the Spanish-American War, the Stars and Stripes now flew over protectorates in the Pacific Ocean as well as the Caribbean. When the vainglorious war hero Colonel Teddy Roosevelt became president in 1901, he feared no man or nation and catapulted the United States' strengths onto the world stage. He brokered the end of the Sino-Japanese War and earned the Nobel Peace Prize for his efforts.

Teddy Roosevelt encouraged and militarily cajoled Panama's secession from Columbia. He magnanimously built the Panama Canal without approval. He enforced the territorial Monroe Doctrine. If a nation or some foreign interest conflicted with his opinion of foreign policy, it received his "big stick" diplomacy. Taken from an African proverb, "Speak softly and carry a big stick, you will go far" defined Teddy Roosevelt's authority for the United States of America to become the "world's policeman"

Cousin Franklin had served as assistant secretary of the navy under Wilson and later was a witnessing emissary to the devastating aftermath of the Great War. When the smoldering embers from that conflict ignited into the second European confrontation during his presidency, FDR, and the nation, were unwilling to get involved. His domestic economic recovery programs had entrenched America into a nation of self-serving isolationists.

As most presidential second terms are seldom as inspiring as the first, FDR developed a legislative disconnect on Capitol Hill; his battles with the Supreme Court remained legendary; and the national economy was taking a well-needed recuperative deep breath from its exhaustive recovery.

"Our full energies may now be released to invigorate the process of recovery in order to preserve our reforms," FDR stated, as if to say it was time for the national herd to graze.

Conversely, on the European continent, Hitler's Third Reich was snatching up nations without resistance or consequence. Austria was annexed as part of Germany, as was a German section of Czechoslovakia. He wantonly and defiantly broke treaties and marched his Nazi armies across western Europe. In Italy, his fellow Axis member Benito Mussolini was heading south into Africa.

In Asia, the Japanese Empire, the third leg of the stool, was attacking the Soviet Union and China for the second time within the century. As the world dealt with its economic issues, Japan was expanding its military presence deep into the Pacific Rim, and no one was doing a thing to stop it.

Roosevelt, on the other hand, was better informed and more philosophically objective than our former European allies. He warned the American people about the risks of neutrality and isolationism. During his Democratic Convention acceptance speech for a second term in 1936, titled, "This Generation Has a Rendezvous with Destiny" he stated, "I believe in my heart that only our success can stir their ancient hope. They begin to know that here in America we are waging a great and successful war. It is not alone a war against want and destitution and economic demoralization. It is more than that; it is a war for the survival of democracy. We are fighting to save a great and precious form of government for ourselves and for the world."

During his State of the Union address in 1939, he reiterated another section from that speech, an ominous prediction of things to come: "There comes a time in the affairs of men when they must prepare to defend not their homes alone but the tenets of faith and humanity on which their churches, their governments, and their very civilization are founded. The defense of religion, of democracy, and of good faith among nations is all the same fight. To save one we must now make up our minds to save all."

Weeks later FDR asked Congress for $525 million to strengthen naval and air defenses. Congress defiantly remained isolationist and fought his military expenditure requests in spite of the increased benefits to the economy. If there were any doubts about their resolve, Congress had the backing of the American people: a poll determined that 77 percent of the American people sought neutrality, even if Britain and France were defeated.[3]

Franklin Roosevelt continued stockpiling naval ships, air force fighters, weapons, and military transport preparing for war under the auspices that we were improving the economy.

When the Nazis invaded Poland, France and Great Britain finally awoken to the realization they were entrée and dessert, respectively, on Hitler's maniacal menu. The two finally declared war on Germany in September 1939. Europe was at war with Germany for the second time in thirty years.

In the spring of 1940, Hitler invaded Norway, the Netherlands, and Belgium. Roosevelt asked Congress for more planes. When France fell to the Nazis in the summer

---

3 The American Heritage Pictorial History of the Presidents of the United States, Vol.2, American Heritage Publishing Co., Inc. 1968, p. 807.

of 1940, Roosevelt finally broke neutrality and started leasing outdated US destroyers to Great Britain in exchange for its naval bases around the North Atlantic basin. In September he instituted a peacetime draft. Roosevelt was clearly preparing for war.

In November 1940 Roosevelt sought an unprecedented third term as president while promising, "Your boys are not going to be sent to any foreign war." He won the election, but Hitler had already begun the massive air assault with the Battle of Britain. During his year-end fireside chat, Roosevelt announced to the nation that America was becoming "the arsenal of Democracy."

In January 1941, he kept up his pressure on Congress, and like Wilson, called for world order, invoking the "four freedoms": freedom of speech, freedom of worship, freedom from want, and freedom from fear. He implored Congress to extend the "lend-lease" program to our other allies. Roosevelt established military and naval bases in Greenland, ordered a strategic bomber program, and established the office of Civilian Defense.

When a German submarine sunk an American destroyer, Roosevelt shuttered the German Embassy and consulates in the United States and froze their assets. He seized German ships harbored in US ports and declared a national emergency. When Hitler invaded the Soviet Union, Roosevelt extended the lend-lease program to them, sent US troops to relieve British troops in Iceland, and folded the Philippine army into the US Armed Forces.

Stalin, Roosevelt & Churchill

Courtesy of the Franklin D. Roosevelt Presidential Library

In August, Roosevelt met with British Prime Minister Winston Churchill, and signed the Atlantic Charter, the precursor of the United Nations. These two leaders, along with their unlikely ally Joseph Stalin, premier of the Soviet Union, would become the "Big Three" allies of World War II.

On December 7, 1941, Japan attacked the United States air-base in Pearl Harbor, Hawaii—"a day that shall live in infamy," articulated Roosevelt before Congress, which authorized the United States to declare war on Japan. In response, Germany and Italy declared war on us, and again the United States found itself engulfed in a world war.

After Pearl Harbor there was overwhelming patriotism in the United States. Most able-bodied men enlisted in the armed services. The ones who did not get shipped off to war remained stateside to aid in the war effort. The wives and mothers stayed home raising the kids. Other women did their part in service to the country or replaced the men in the workplace.

My father evolved his medical bookstore into a surgical sup-ply enterprise. During the depression, he extended credit to the medical students and interns, saying, "When you become a big-time doctor, come back and give me your business," and they all did. He was on his way to becoming New England's largest medical supply dealer when the war broke out.

Since he was the breadwinner for the family and had practi-cal knowledge of medical supplies, after he was drafted the US Army thought it better for him to remain stateside and work at a medical supply distribution center in Georgia. He agreed and decided to marry my mother before he left. He was thirty years old, after all, and it was time for him to settle down.

Just before Christmas 1942, my parents were wed and enjoyed a three-day honeymoon at Mount Vernon. My father left by train after the honeymoon, but not before leaving my mother in the family way. She remained in her childhood home with her widowed mother and siblings to have his baby. She did not see my father again until Thanksgiving of 1943, just enough time to meet his son, visit with his own family, and knock her up for the second time. By the following Christmas, he had obtained a transfer to Fort Dix in New Jersey and spent the holiday with his wife, and their two sons.

When it was decided that he would stay at his mother-in-law's house, my grandmother asked my mother what he liked to eat. My mother replied she had no idea. She had spent only a total of five days with him in the past two years and could not really remember much about him!

These were the unreal sacrifices that US citizens made in those days. Most of the folks who endured them will recall days of food and gasoline rationing or of being sent away from home for the first time, on a ship to some Godforsaken place on earth no one would want to visit even without a rifle, never knowing if they would return to their wife or mother.

Over four hundred thousand Americans gave their lives for freedom and liberty in World War II. Combined with the previous war, that is over half a million sons and daughters slaughtered by strangers in wars we had no business in, but for the fact we were the "world's policeman"

5

WHO THE HELL IS HARRY TRUMAN?

In 1944, when Franklin Roosevelt decided to run for a fourth term, it was visually obvious that the historical events of his three terms as president were having a debilitating effect on his health. Not only was he aging from the physiological stress of the office, but the degenerative complications of a chain-smoking, paralytically wheelchair-bound man of his age were raising health warnings from his medical advisers. His political advisers were also rightfully concerned, and not just of his personal well-being.

Democratic leaders were worried that, if the inevitable were to happen during Roosevelt's fourth term, Vice President Henry Wallace—who occasionally demonstrated unstable behavior—was not a suitable constitutional successor, either as a wartime commander in chief or later as an effective peace-time negotiator. They began to search for a replacement on the party's ticket.

After much handwringing, they selected Harry S. Truman, a well-respected senator from Missouri. Truman, a former haberdasher from Kansas City, was unknown to many, Roosevelt included. In fact, the war-worn Roosevelt didn't even know Truman's résumé until the convention. Yet the ever-loyal Democrat agreed with the party leaders, and soon enough Truman was Roosevelt's third vice president. Few suspected, especially Truman, that Roosevelt's health would deteriorate so rapidly and he would die just four months after his fourth inauguration.

Truman & Roosevelt

Office of War Information, courtesy of the Harry S. Truman Library.

One afternoon while presiding over the Senate, Truman was summoned to the White House by Mrs. Roosevelt, who delivered the grim report of Franklin's death. After receiving the stunning news, a shocked Truman, after coming to grips that he was now the nation's thirty-third president, asked Mrs. Roosevelt if there was anything he could do for her. She responded, "Is there anything we can do for you? For you are the one in trouble now."

Not a joyous declaration from the first lady, but a harsh reality. Truman was now the most powerful man in the world and profoundly ill suited for the job. He knew very little of the inner workings of the three-term Roosevelt White House. He was also an inexperienced and uninformed commander in chief suddenly thrown into the depths of a complicated global military engagement. Additionally, he was oblivious to the delicate and exhaustive negotiations of the Big Three conferences with Churchill and Stalin.

The European war ended just a few weeks after Truman assumed the presidency, on his sixty-first birthday. Truman's first act as a postwar president was to travel to Potsdam, Germany, for a summit with Churchill and Stalin to discuss the Nazi surrender, postwar Europe, and the defeat of the Japanese empire.

Had Roosevelt considered his moral obligation or the professional accountability to brief the new vice president on the details of previous Allied Conferences at Tehran and Yalta, or the existence of the atomic bomb, Truman may have had a better grasp of the approaching powwow at the Potsdam Conference. But Roosevelt had not. As a result, Truman was able to quickly ascertain the illegitimacy of Joseph Stalin. Truman's fresh eyes and ears worked to his advantage, which may have been Roosevelt's plan, but we will never know, or understand, why an ailing FDR kept Truman in the dark.

Stalin was a strict Leninist and a Bolshevik revolutionary who fought in the October Uprising of 1917 to overthrow Czar Nicholas II. From 1922 until his death in 1952, Stalin was the general secretary, the grand Pooh-Bah, of the Communist Party in the Soviet Union. Stalin signed a nonaggression pact with the Nazis in 1939 to regain dominance over pre-WWI Soviet-controlled nations. When Hitler broke the pact and attacked the Soviet Union, Stalin joined the Allies and invaded Nazi Germany on the eastern front.

Stalin, however, was a vicious totalitarian tyrant. On his watch, 1.7 million Soviets died in work camps (gulags), eight hundred thousand were executed for political or criminal offenses, four hundred thousand died in resettlement programs, 158,000 soldiers were executed for desertion, and millions of civilians perished due to famine and illness. Stalin was a no-good son of a bitch, but he was a necessary evil to defeat the Nazis.

To make matters worse, the Potsdam Conference was disrupted by a sequence of bizarre events. First, Churchill was ousted as prime minister by a British midwar election that removed his party, and therefore him, from government. Go figure. Secondly,

Stalin announced that he had annexed Poland and established a communist government there and was planning to do the same in a number of other Baltic states. The Western leaders balked, yet Stalin claimed these nations to be a "buffer zone" to prevent future attacks. The United States and Great Britain were given little choice but to acquiesce. Thirdly, Truman learned to distrust Stalin. When Truman shared the news that the United States had developed the atomic bomb, Stalin remained nonplussed and unimpressed. Truman correctly ascertained that Stalin was previously informed of its existence as a result of Soviet espionage within the United States. The Potsdam Conference was the first frost of the impending Cold War.

The Allies did concur that with the defeat of the Nazis and ensuing peace in Europe, all combined military efforts should be redirected to end the war in the Pacific theater. Furthermore, if the Japanese refused to surrender, the Allies mutually agreed to permit the use of the US atomic bombs to persuade them to do so.

When the Japanese ignored the Allies' first request to surrender, Truman sent a second, more properly worded diplomatic ultimatum threatening an attack of cataclysmic consequences if they did not immediately agree to lay down their arms. Again, there was no response.

Truman ordered the atomic bomb "Little Boy" to be dropped on Hiroshima, evaporating over one hundred thousand Japanese citizens. Crickets. Three days later he dropped another atomic bomb, the "Fat Man," on Nagasaki, killing another eighty thousand people. That caught their attention. Not knowing how many more atomic bombs the United States possessed, Japan agreed to unconditionally surrender. Truman never regretted his decision to drop the bomb, for he assumed it saved one hundred thousand US military lives and it was Christian morality overcoming evil.

"The atom bomb was no 'great decision.' It was merely another powerful weapon in the arsenal of righteousness," Truman stated.

The United States may have been the sole superpower as the world entered the Atomic Age, but there was much more to be accomplished. Truman needed to lobby the governments of the world to collectively agree to establish the United Nations as a promoter of peace and a deterrent of war, as the planet would not survive another global conflict.

Fulfilling Wilson's dream of a League of Nations, the United Nations was founded in 1945. Its architects envisioned a unilateral organization that would act to prevent conflicts between nations and make future wars impossible. However, the outbreak of the Cold War made peacekeeping agreements extremely difficult as the geopolitical divisions of the globe were partitioned into hostile camps.

The Allied agreements from the Yalta Conference also contained "mandates" that should be placed under United Nations trusteeship once the war was over. The most notable mandate was a parcel of land in the Middle East known as Palestine. Occupied by the British since the fall of the Ottoman Empire in WWI, the cash-poor British government sought to purge itself of its financial responsibility in Palestine.

Truman worried that the "Holy Land" would become violent in absence of British control. He was correct.

When Britain announced its intention to prematurely exit Palestine, the Jewish leadership, led by future Israeli Prime Minister David Ben-Gurion, instantly pounced and seized both the land and the opportunity to declare an independent State of Israel. In an act of solidarity and to prevent future turmoil, the United States and the Soviet Union quickly recognized Israel. However, Israel was not recognized by neighboring Arab states, which promptly invaded the new nation to claim disputed and historic borders. After a year of anarchy and battle, the State of Israel was accepted as a member of the United Nations by majority vote in May 1949.

"I had faith in Israel before it was established," Truman said. "I have faith in it now. I believe it has a glorious future before it—not just another sovereign nation, but as an embodiment of the great ideals of our civilization."

Truman continued his empathy for the Jewish people. When in postwar Europe the atrocities of the concentration camps were exposed, especially the ungodly genocide and diabolical treatment of the Jewish race at the hands of the Nazis, Truman demanded that the major war criminals be subjected to a judicial process held in a world court in Nuremberg, Germany.

When some suggested that the world be spared the spectacle of the heinous treatment and the hideous crimes against humanity within the concentration camps, Truman disagreed. He wanted to document and expose the brutality and savagery for the entire world to witness, as well as dispel any future accusations that claims about the camps were mere Allied propaganda.

In spite of Truman's efforts, contemporary Holocaust skeptics and anti-Semites continue to dispute these facts. In the end, eleven war criminals were hanged, three were acquitted, and three were given life sentences. Others were given extended sentences of incarceration. Two cowards emulated their leader and committed suicide. The acknowledgment of their names does not belong here, or printed anywhere for that matter, with the exception of the gates to hell.

In the post-Potsdam world, Truman's suspicions of Stalin proved correct. Stalin was accumulating nations to fortify the Soviet Union's Eastern Bloc. He also refused to vacate Iran on the date agreed to in the Potsdam Treaty. Additionally there was the issue with Greece and Turkey. Truman proclaimed, "I'm tired of babying the Soviets."

As with Palestine, Britain had been supporting Greece for years, but in its post-WWII economy, it could do longer afford to do so. The British reached out to Truman, stating that if Greece fell to the Soviets, Turkey would soon follow, potentially causing a "domino effect" in the region. Once again Truman agreed with the Brits and rose to the occasion, asking the now Republican-controlled Congress for $400 million to "contain" the Soviets. Congress wholeheartedly agreed. Thus, the Truman Doctrine of "communist containment" and the Cold War officially began.

Later, the North Atlantic Treaty Organization, or NATO, which consisted of eleven nations and the United States, banded together and proclaimed that any act of aggression on any one of the member nations was an act of war against all. Both Turkey and Greece were invited to join, forever ending the chance of Soviet domination in the area. Stalin countered NATO with the "Iron Curtain" of Soviet-dominated nations.

Next, Congress funded Truman's $12 billion Marshall Plan to rebuild Europe and restore industry and trade. In the final year of its four-year objective, the economies of every nation that accepted assistance were running ahead of prewar levels. By the 1952 output, they had surpassed prewar levels by 35 percent, and Europe enjoyed a generation of unmatched prosperity. In an act of goodwill by Truman, he invited the Soviet Union and its satellites to participate in the Marshall Plan, but they declined, and as a result their economies continued to sputter and fail.

The Soviets were so embarrassed and embittered by the enthusiastic European response to the generosity of the United States that Stalin played his last card against Truman and blockaded access to West Berlin, a city deep within Soviet-occupied East Germany. Truman was not bothered; he ordered the goods flown in by military transport, knowing full well that Stalin would not open fire on US planes. By the conclusion of the "Berlin Airlift," the Western powers were delivering five thousand tons of food, medical supplies, and candy bars each day to the sequestered city, further embarrassing Stalin and the Soviet Union. The broken eggs that Stalin used to brag were necessary to make a revolutionary omelet were now firmly affixed to his mustachioed face.

Although Truman was winning the public relations effort in Europe, he was having a difficult time on the home front. The domestic postwar economy was lagging. Somehow the nationalistic and patriotic virtues that endured throughout the war were now waning at home when it came to individual finances. Truman lost the Democratic majority in Congress in 1946, the first time since 1930.

Truman had to deal with coal strikes, railroad strikes, severe shortages, and the Taft-Hartley Act. Passed by the Republican Congress, Taft-Hartley reduced the power of labor unions, proud supporters of all things Democratic since Wilson. Truman vetoed the bill, but it was overridden by Congress and became law. Although initially an embarrassment for Truman, it remains in effect today and ironically has worked both as a malady and a remedy for Democratic presidents.

As Truman prepared for the election in 1948, he sought to establish himself as a true Democrat, embracing Roosevelt's New Deal, proposing nationalized medical coverage, desegregating the armed forces, and promoting Civil Rights legislation.

"The compelling motive in my decision to run for the presidency in 1948 was the same as it had been in 1944. There was still 'unfinished business,' " he said.

The voters had grown weary of the Democrats. Southern "Dixiecrats," Democrats who supported states' rights and opposed Truman's desegregation policies, attempted to split the party. As an incumbent but never-elected president, Truman needed to address his nation. He headed out from Washington by train, out into the hinterlands, crisscrossing the nation on a thirty thousand mile "whistle-stop tour." Truman drew millions of admirers out from the kitchens of the country, delivering up to eight speeches a day. A New York City ticker tape parade produced over a million spectators.

Although the press projected his opponent, New York Governor Thomas Dewey, a man my father always said looked like "the bridegroom on the wedding cake," as the winner, "Give 'em Hell Harry" carried the day. Along with his reelection, Truman brought in the Democratic Freshman Class of 1948 to Congress, making Congress Democratic again and establishing the Democratic Party as the nation's majority party for the next twenty years.

Once Truman was reelected, he got back to business, proclaiming the "Buck Stops Here"—meaning that there was no more passing the buck and that all the unsolved problems of the nation would eventually land on his desk, and he would handle them.

"A president either is constantly on top of events or, if he hesitates, events will soon be on top of him," Truman said. "I never felt that I could let up for a moment. "

The one issue that would never leave Truman's side was communism. It was multidimensional. He fought it and contained it in Europe. He also fought it at home, during Senator Joseph McCarthy's infamous Red Scare and the House's Committee on Un-American Activities hearings, which he abhorred. He addressed the burden when he created the Central Intelligence Agency, or CIA. In 1950 he fought communism again, this time in Asia.

An offshoot of the Potsdam Treaty was the division of the Korean Peninsula. After the Japanese surrender, the Korean Peninsula was divided at the 38th Parallel. The Soviet Union controlled the North, the United States the South. After a series of failed elections, the North embraced a Soviet-sponsored form of communism, and the South adapted a United States form of democracy. After many attempts to reunite the peninsula and numerous border skirmishes, the North invaded the South. The situation went before the United Nations Security Council for resolution. The Soviet Union could have avoided an armed conflict, but it boycotted the Security Council meeting and war broke out.

American troops, assisted by UN military forces, pushed the North Koreans back above the 38th Parallel—and then some for good measure. This enraged the Red Chinese, who began to offer military supplies to their fellow Asian communists and pushed US forces back below the 38th Parallel.

This back and forth went on for a while and eventually ended in a stalemate. Finally a Demilitarized Zone (DMZ) was established and peace was restored; yet the Korean War remains the first conflict of the Cold War, with over thirty-five thousand Americans sacrificing their lives to prevent the communists from overtaking the peninsula. The DMZ remains in effect today, and North Korea continues to be governed by a communist dictator and does not enjoy a formal diplomatic relationship with the United States.

About the same time, Vietnam declared its independence from France. The United States wanted France to "contain" the spread of communism into Indochina, but as usual, France was too self-absorbed to take on the task. As a result, it declared Vietnam a lost cause and vacated the country in 1953.

My father's family was spared much involvement in WWII. His "kid brother" of fourteen years, Uncle Jim, returned after serving one year as a signalman in the navy, but as a veteran, he was entitled to receive the benefits of the Servicemen's Readjustment Act.

"The GI Bill", as it became known, was enacted in June 1944. Franklin Roosevelt wanted something to benefit vets returning from military service, and Congress concurred. All former servicemen were entitled to zero-down, low-interest home mortgages. This allowed the veterans to vacate urban apartments and move to suburbia. Veterans were also entitled to receive twenty dollars a week for a year while they looked for work. Less than 20 percent of the funds allocated were ever used, as most vets quickly found jobs or pursued an education.

In the case of my Uncle Jim, his high school grades and athletic accomplishments were good enough for him to be accepted to Harvard College and make the varsity football team as a freshman. My father, who had given up his college career to fend for the family, lived vicariously through his younger brother's athletic achievements.

Harvard College had been a haven for the descendants of the *Mayflower* and the affluent, but the post-WWII campus became a melting pot of cultures and ethnic backgrounds. My uncle, the son of Irish immigrants, played football at Harvard with Sam Adams, a spawn of the famous US revolutionary family. He played with Jews, sons of Italian and Polish immigrants, and the first northern African-American to play football south of the Mason-Dixon Line. Other sons of noble Irish heritage were captains Ken and Cleo O'Donnell and a spunky little kid named Bobby Kennedy.

This group of guys would make an enormous impact of my father's association with the Democratic Party and world affairs, but not my grandfather. He died before he could see his sons flourish in post-World War II affluence. He died of a heart attack one day doing a menial job, just attempting to stay busy.

In true Irish tradition, he was never spoken of again. I used to ask my father about his dad, but he told me only a few things: He had beautiful blue eyes, he played the flute, he never drank alcohol until he lost his job on the B&M Railroad, and he thought that Franklin Roosevelt was the greatest man in the world.

6

IKE & THE COLD WAR

Although Harry Truman did not seek reelection in 1952, he encouraged the president of Columbia University, Dwight D. "Ike" Eisenhower, to run in the election of 1952. General Eisenhower, the former supreme commander of the Allied Forces in Europe and NATO, took Truman's advice and pursued the office of president—but did so as a Republican. The two decades of the New Deal coalition by the Democrats had come to a close.

A five-star general from West Point, Ike ran on a platform to end the Korean War, destroy communism, and expose corruption. Having witnessed enough war for a lifetime, Ike sought to make the 1950s a time for peace and prosperity in America. His military training and experience made him too uncommunicative and disinterested to deal with the intricacies of diplomacy and politics. He would rather rattle the atomic saber of his nuclear arsenal at the slightest provocation than send troops into battle. When the Korean conflict dragged on a little too long, Ike threatened the Chinese with nuclear war. They folded like a cheap church chair, and the war was over.

To reduce defense spending and thus federal deficits, Eisenhower opted to build up the American arsenal of affordable nuclear weapons, all the while keeping financial pressure of the Soviet Union to fund its nuclear deterrence program. Unexpectedly, the Soviets pulled a fast one on Ike and launched the satellite *Sputnik* into the earth's orbit, catching the United States off guard and replacing the arms race with the space race.

An opponent of the glacial process of congressional legislation, Ike's decisions were prepared as the commander in chief, not the chief executive, and he made up his mind quickly and succinctly. Having never held political office, Ike was neither a political animal nor indebted to any politicians. Ike left the day-to-day political minutiae in the capable hands of his vice president, Richard Nixon, a former congressman and senator.

Ike's greatest achievements as president were the expansion of Social Security benefits and the building of the interstate highway system, which he justified as a defensive maneuver, saying metropolitan cities were vulnerable to foreign attacks. The new highways greatly benefited Detroit's auto industry and changed the social fabric of the prosperous nation. Ike also sent federal troops to Little Rock, Arkansas, to enforce federal court orders to desegregate public schools. In spite of the political necessity of Nixon, Ike did not suffer fools lightly, and a decade of peace and prosperity encapsulated a simpler time.

The Eisenhower administration did have its failings. Besides playing catch-up in the space race, Ike's efforts to secure a summit with the Soviet Union collapsed when a U-2 reconnaissance plane was shot down over Russia. The incident left him exposed and embarrassed and forced Ike to negotiate with the infuriated Soviets for the pilot's safe return. Ike also underestimated Fidel Castro in Soviet-backed Cuba and ignored the French warnings to avoid involvement in Indochina, most notably Vietnam.

Ike also utilized the CIA to overthrow a number of governments in order gain respect and garner fear in the geopolitical theater of global dominance.

Ike was a sometime an absentee president, playing more golf than governing or recovering from repeated heart attacks.

As Norman Mailer observed in his 1960 political analysis *Superman Comes to the Supermarket;* "But since America has been passing through a period of enormous expansion since the war, the double-four years of Dwight Eisenhower could not retard the expansion, it could only denude it of color, character, and the development of novelty." [4]

Vice President Richard Nixon attempted to keep the White House Republican and ran a strong campaign against the Democratic nominee, Senator John F. Kennedy until he humiliated Nixon in the first televised presidential debate of

---

4 Esquire Magazine, November 1960.

1960. Ike was so fearful of Kennedy's youth and inexperience he stumped heavily for Nixon in the waning days of the campaign, but it was too little too late, and Kennedy won the general election by a tenth of a percentage point.

Eisenhower was so alarmed at Kennedy's naiveté that he warned the nation of the Cold War realities of communism in his farewell speech to the nation, just a few days before Kennedy assumed his office.

"We face a hostile ideology global in scope, atheistic in character, ruthless in purpose and insidious in method," he said.

It would not be long before Kennedy was faced with Eisenhower's prophecy and planned to demonstrate his ability in the world theater.

7

THE VETERANS

Thanks to the GI Bill, nearly eight million veterans either attended college or enrolled in an employment-training program. When the vets entered the workforce, they created the most unique and most envied civilization of modern times: the American middle class. It remains a socioeconomic phenomenon that exhibits both Roosevelt's genius and the idiomatic aptitude of the American worker. Roosevelt anticipated future generations as an income tax base that would not only fund his social programs but also form a middle class that would stimulate economic growth and create a consumer-driven society.

As the GI Bill sponsored and promoted home ownership, 2.4 million veterans attained low-interest, federally funded mortgages, and the housing markets boomed. "Levittown" neighborhoods sprung up almost overnight. New homes were chock full of modern home appliances and television sets. The suburban labor force purchased automobiles to commute back and forth to work. Later, the growing family bought a second car, usually station wagons, for moms to drive to the supermarket and families to use on vacations on the nation's new highway system. "See the USA in a Chevrolet" was the mantra, and they traveled from New England to California. No culture had ever lived like this before. Americans drove their cars to dine at drive-in restaurants and to watch films at drive-in movie theaters.

Post-WWII families had children, lots of them. Sixty-six million children were born between 1946 and 1964. These were kids who went to doctors' offices for vaccines and medical care and to dentists to straighten their teeth. They bought toys and bicycles to get around when mom was out driving her station wagon, buying groceries for the neighborhood barbecue party.

These kids attended newly built schools during the week, joined the Boy and Girl Scouts, played on Little League teams, and attended church programs on the weekends. They watched shows on television about people who looked and lived like them. They were the "baby boomer generation", and they were everywhere.

My nuclear family was part of this generation and enjoyed most of the comforts that went along with it. By the time my Uncle Jim got out of Harvard, most of my father's relatives had married and settled in our hometown of Brookline, Massachusetts.

My father's business was doing well; he was raising his younger siblings, with guidance from his mother, on the same street that my mother was raising his. My father attempted to slow down a little and relax more, playing golf on the week-ends and going to Cape Cod in the summer.

One of Brookline's town elders approached my father about an opening on the school committee and encouraged him to run. Initially he was not interested. The old sage pushed him, pointing out that the town had educated him, a bunch of siblings, a few of his children, and dozens of nephews and nieces, and it was time to give back. The elder added that civic participation and politics would make him a better man. My now-enlightened father agreed, threw his hat in the ring, and won the election.

Soon afterward, two of Uncle Jim's teammates from the Harvard football team appeared at my father's doorstep. Kenny O'Donnell and Bobby Kennedy were managing the campaign for Kennedy's older brother, a congressman who now sought to be a US senator. They stated they needed my father's assistance in Brookline. At first my father balked, thinking it would be better for Uncle Jim to serve the position; they were his friends, after all. The two young Turks responded that Jim Noonan had no interest in politics and had sent them to see my father. The old man was trapped.

O'Donnell and Kennedy explained how they planned to start a grassroots campaign and entice locally elected officials to work his city or town, as a nonpaid "secretary." If they could depend on each secretary to win over the local constituents, they could win the statewide election and eventually turn

Massachusetts Democratic, wresting control of it from the puritanical Republican Brahmins. My father was sold. He had been subjected to Irish Catholic bigotry by that bunch. But first he had to meet the candidate. When he did, they became fast friends and political allies.

Jack Kennedy was a well-educated, well-decorated war veteran, with a well-financed campaign. When Kennedy initially sought national political office from Boston, it was a city his ancestors knew well but of which he knew very little. Kennedy was well accustomed to the parlor games of the city's elite and the social clubs of Harvard, but not the ethnic neighborhoods. He needed local color to help him connect with the voters, the common man.

Kennedy recruited a local personality named Dave Powers from Charlestown to show him around his future congressional precinct. Powers successfully taught him how to relate to blue-collar workers in the ethnic neighborhoods. Kennedy won that 1946 congressional election, taking Powers with him to be his friend, keep him grounded, and to remind him of the importance of the common man.

Now, six years later, Congressman Kennedy took on a wildly popular and highly revered member of the Massachusetts Republican Party, US Senator Henry Cabot Lodge Jr., the namesake of Woodrow Wilson's nemesis.

"And this is good old Boston,

The home of the bean and the cod,

Where the Lowells talk only to Cabots,

And the Cabots talk only to God." [5]

These Cabots and Lodges had been serving in Congress since the beginning of the republic. They never took any Democrat seriously; they never had to, especially a contender in Massachusetts politics. Lodge decided instead to manage General Eisenhower's Republican presidential campaign in 1952, completely dismissing the young Jack Kennedy and his grassroots campaign. Lodge was caught sleeping.

In spite of a national Republican landslide, Kennedy defeated Lodge, becoming only the third Democrat ever elected US senator from Massachusetts. Years later, after some internal Massachusetts Democratic Party drama, Kennedy became the leading Democrat in the commonwealth and encouraged my father to run for selectman in their hometown of Brookline. My father agreed and with Kennedy's support won the election.

My parents, much to their surprise, were expecting my arrival in the spring of 1958. Apparently my father was a little overwhelmed that year with his campaign, Kennedy's reelection

5 Anonymous.

campaign, the stress of running a business, and coming home to a wife exhausted from rearing three teenagers, a five-year-old, and a newborn. By November he was pretty stressed out. When a young Democratic town meeting member gave him some mouth music about campaigning within fifty feet of a voting booth, my father finally lost his cool and gave the "little shin kicker" a good thump.

My father won his election, and Kennedy won his reelection with the largest plurality of votes ever attained by any candidate in Massachusetts history. With the wind at their backs, the Kennedy political team pragmatically surveyed the national political landscape, gauged how Kennedy's national image compared with his contemporaries, and decided he was a credible presidential candidate in 1960.

Asking "Why not me? If not now, when?" Kennedy declared himself a candidate for president of the United States in January 1960. He was forty-two years old. After a contentious series of Democratic primaries, where Kennedy's Catholicism, his father's financial influence, and his implied inexperience were called into question, Kennedy persevered.

My father was selected as a delegate from the Bay State and, with my mother, headed west to the Democratic National Convention in Los Angeles to watch Kennedy win the nomination on an unprecedented first ballot. The next day Kennedy selected Senate Majority Leader Lyndon Johnson from Texas as his running mate, much to the chagrin of his political team, which was still managed by Kenny O'Donnell and Bobby Kennedy, whom loathed Johnson.

With Kennedy winning on the first ballot, the Massachusetts delegation decided to take a bus ride, with wives, to Las Vegas for a little fun. It must have been the extreme desert heat that caused the bus to break down. It must have been the same heat that caused the parched Irishmen to produce a few bottles of whiskey. It must have been the whiskey that caused the delegates to break into song, Kennedy campaign jingles, and emotional Irish ballads, but by the time a replacement bus arrived, they were a cemented group of Massachusetts Irish Catholics, dubbed by the press as the "Irish Mafia." Collectively they were on the way to the White House and none, including my parents, whose photograph adorned the front page of the *Boston Globe*, could have been happier.

This was my Father's Democratic Party. All their hard work, late nights, internal party struggles, and endless cups of tea would be for naught if they could not defeat Richard Nixon in November. Kennedy took him to the cleaners at every opportunity, even in humor.

"Do you realize the responsibility I carry? I'm the only person who stands between Nixon and the White House."

When Nixon tried to give it back to Kennedy, recalling how as vice president he shook his finger in Soviet Premier Nikita Khrushchev's face in their infamous "kitchen debate,"

Kennedy quipped, "Mr. Nixon may be very experienced in kitchen debates, but so are many other husbands I know."

The compelling advantage for Kennedy was the four televised presidential debates. Kennedy appeared visually, intellectually, and presidentially astute in stark comparison with the heavily perspiring, nervous, and ashen-faced Nixon.

"I don't run for the office of the presidency to tell you what you want to hear," Kennedy said during a campaign swing through Maine. "I run for the office of the presidency because in dangerous times we need to be told what we must do if we are going to maintain freedom and the freedom of those who depend on us."

It was a tough election, yet Kennedy pulled it off with the slightest margin. The candidate's father, Joseph P. Kennedy, had once declared, "All you need is 51 percent of the vote. The rest doesn't matter."

Kennedy was able to provide only 49.7 percent of the vote, one-tenth of a percent more than Nixon, who won more states but not enough of the electoral votes. Nixon declined requests by Republican leaders for a recount.

Kennedy's presidential election slogan was a "Man for the 60's". He may have known that the 1960s were going to be a historic decade, but he had no possible idea how profoundly his administration would leave its mark on it.

8

KENNEDY, CUBA, & THE COMMIES

John F. Kennedy was the first president born in the twentieth century. He was also the youngest man ever elected president and the first Roman Catholic. Although he was raised in wealth, his life was not without strife. Kennedy had near-death experiences more than once in his life. Occurrences of this dimension forever change the survivors' attitude. I know—I've had a few myself. Some become more religious, some become more fearless. Either way, they become more courageous after having witnessed their own mortality and cheated death. Kennedy was one of these survivors, fatalistic at times, but a realist who understood what is important in life and who knew how to align his objectives in the pursuit of happiness.

In January 1961, Kennedy took his presidential oath and delivered the most notable and easily the most quotable inaugural addresses since George Washington. Most scholars and historians remember Kennedy's iconic call to domestic service with his rendition of a preparatory school's motto: "Ask not what your country can do for you; ask what you can do for your country."

What most do not recall, is that at the height of the Cold War, Kennedy warned communist aggressors that he would be no pushover: "Let every nation know, whether it wishes us well or ill, that we shall pay any price, bear any burden, meet any hardship, support any friend, oppose any foe, to assure the survival and the success of liberty."

To postwar Democrats, the Kennedy White House is their proudest and most celebrated administration. Kennedy's iconic style was an amalgamation of good looks, true intellect, and inspirational vision. Erudite as Wilson, provocative as Roosevelt, and pragmatic as Truman, Kennedy was a realist and a free thinker who sought to bring energy and optimism to his administration, dubbing it the "New Frontier".

Kennedy refined and modernized the office of president. He acted as the hub of his administration, having all ideas brought to him. He employed no chief of staff, yet kept Powers, O'Donnell, and brother Bobby as close to him as possible, all for specific and inimitable reasons.

Along with his cultured wife and young children, the Kennedys brought youth and elegance to the once-dowdy White House. They embraced American arts, music, and culture. They also redefined the ceremonial protocol of the office, making it more grandiose while more comfortable for foreign dignitaries. Even the White House limousine fleet of funereal-black Cadillacs was replaced with navy blue Lincoln Continentals, some convertible. They hired a designer to fashion a new motif and color combinations for the new livery of presidential jets. They entertained Noble Prize winners, artists, musicians, and poets, and they exhibited treasures and preserved architecture. They did it all.

Now, as an obvious departure from the austere and grandfatherly Eisenhower, the avuncular president called for volunteerism and nationalism from the nation's youth. The "Kennedy Kids" responded to his challenge for civil rights for minorities at home and enlisted in his two-year international mission of the Peace Corps. During the primary process, Kennedy may have denied that Rome would have an effect on his administration, but he was sure governing like a Jesuit missionary.

Kennedy signed executive orders increasing aid to unemployed Americans and bringing food stamps, welfare assistance, and housing to the poor. He increased the minimum wage for workers, fought racial discrimination in the workplace, and assisted farmers. He halted water pollution, expanded mass transportation projects, and created national parks. He asked Congress to include health insurance in the Social Security program and initiated the space race to the Moon. He addressed Congress, proclaiming the United States would within a decade send man to the moon and return him safely to earth. His prophecy lacked the technology or even a blueprint to accomplish such a galactic endeavor. All of this was presented in his first year as president. He was, as his wife referred to him, a "whirlwind".

"The United States did not rise to greatness by waiting for others to lead... Economic isolation and political leadership are wholly incompatible." Stated a spirited and optimistic Kennedy.

Under Kennedy, the economic growth of the nation doubled from 3 percent to 6 percent. The four years following his inauguration represented the longest and strongest economic expansion in modern history. The Kennedy administration proposed and passed tax credits encouraging businesses to invest in new machinery and equipment.

Kennedy lowered interest rates and simplified the application criteria for Small Business Administration loans. He took my father out of politics and retirement and appointed him Northeast director of the SBA. When an aide advised Kennedy that my father might not accept the post, JFK sent that aide to my father to relay the comment that "the president thinks this would make you a better man." My father knew Kennedy had recycled the phrase that the Brookline elder had once used to lure him into politics. He accepted the position in Boston, for he wanted to remain in Brookline and not uproot our family to Washington.

Like other kids my age, I would ask my father what he did for work. Unlike other kids my age, my father had an official government car with a telephone. He would attempt to explain how he would make loans for "Uncle Sam" and worked in joint venture with young companies, especially those he called "NASA babies" that were developing new technology for the Moonshot, but it was a little over my head at the time.

Many of the national SBA loans were granted to New England companies, not just because it was Kennedy's corner of the country but also because the Boston-Cambridge area was the technology center of the nation and, at the time, where NASA was based.

Harvard, MIT, and the US Air Force Cambridge Research Laboratory were developing new computers, space guidance systems, instrumentation, optics, and microwave radiation for NASA. These were the commercialized incubators of the NASA babies. Even AT&T built its regional switch location in Cambridge in preparation for the location of mission control. Remember, NASA had only nine years to get an American to the moon and back.

In spite of Kennedy's economic efforts, the stock market made huge swings during his administration. He sought to stabilize the economy by controlling inflation with updated tariffs and personal and corporate tax cuts. He exerted presidential pressure on United States steel companies that proposed price increases. By cutting $10 billion from the federal budget, Kennedy sought a balanced budget in 1963, but he was spending defense funds like a drunken sailor on shore leave.

Militarily, Kennedy began the most rapid peacetime buildup of the nation's defense program in history. He doubled the Polaris (submarine) missile program, increased and improved the armed bomber program, and added five combat-ready antiguerilla forces, among them, the Navy SEALs and the Green Berets.

"We arm to parley", was a Winston Churchill quote Kennedy enjoyed.

Kennedy may have been seeking a "peace race" with the Soviet Union, but similar to Teddy Roosevelt, he planned to negotiate with the big stick of military strength.

Kennedy was stern with the communists on foreign policy issues. He warned the Soviets about interfering with the United Nations in Africa, sought peace negotiations with Red China in Southeast Asia, and proactively established the anti communist Alliance of Progress in Latin America. Yet he had stumbled badly in Cuba.

In his first one hundred days in office, Kennedy had been stung for authorizing a CIA-orchestrated, Eisenhower-approved, and mercenary-led invasion of Soviet-sponsored Cuba. Known as the Bay of Pigs invasion, the landing went terribly wrong, causing Kennedy to renege on promised US air support. It was an utter failure, giving his "inexperienced" detractors instant fodder and driving an enormous wedge of doubt between the commander in chief and his military forces at the Pentagon. Kennedy took sole responsibility, stating, "Success has many fathers, while failure is an orphan."

The American people may have forgiven him, but not the Cuban exiles in the United States or Cuban President Fidel Castro. A few months later, Kennedy headed to Vienna for a summit with his diplomatic antagonist, Soviet Premier Nikita Khrushchev.

Kennedy & Khrushchev

Courtesy of the John F. Kennedy Presidential Library and Museum

Historically, summits are usually failures, and this one was no exception. Now sitting face-to-face with his opposing nuclear superpower leader, Kennedy was eager to make a strong first impression on Khrushchev. It failed to work, as Kennedy later explained, "He savaged me."

Khrushchev viewed Kennedy as naive, inexperienced, and fearful to fight. Kennedy was not afraid to fight but, like Wilson, was above getting dragged into a futile conflict. In Kennedy's case, the stakes were mutual nuclear annihilation. Their initial engagement regressed into a challenge of wills and concluded without accomplishment or diplomatic agreements.

It did, however, open the channels of teletype communication between the two nations. Kennedy firmly believed that the lack of clarity and communication had led many nations unnecessarily to war, when an open dialogue could have prevented it. So he was pleased at that level, for a short while.

After Vienna and a summer of exhausting and unproductive diplomatic debate, Khrushchev erected the Berlin Wall to keep Eastern Europeans from defecting to the West, making West Berlin a virtual island in a sea of Soviet-controlled East Germany. Although Kennedy loathed the act, there was little he could do without starting a nuclear war. Two years later he stood at the Berlin Wall and proclaimed in his famous "I am a Berliner" speech, "Freedom has many difficulties, and democracy is not perfect, but we have never had to put a wall up to keep our people in."

There was no relief from similar acts of aggression by the communists. All over the globe they were lighting revolutionary brushfires, and Kennedy was running around stomping them out. It had become a game of cat and mouse. Yet all that back and forth came to an abrupt halt in the fall of 1962, when United States intelligence determined that the Soviet Union was placing long-range nuclear missiles in Cuba. "When we got into office, the thing that surprised me the most was that things were as bad as we'd been saying they were." Kennedy stated when he was made cognizant of the Soviet Union's obsession with global domination.

This was really bad. Located ninety miles off the coast of southern Florida, the island of Cuba was a resort for wealthy Americans in the 1950s and had become a dichotomy of haves and have-nots. The puppet government of President Fulgencio Batista (who represented the haves) allowed the capital city, Havana, to become nothing more than an offshore casino for US-based organized crime families and the countryside farmland of sugarcane to be exploited by foreign corporations. Fidel Castro, his communist revolutionaries, and the farm workers (the have-nots) were opposed to the unequal balance of wealth and power and overthrew the government on New Year's Day 1959.

Castro and his communist revolutionaries were both deeply anticapitalist and anti-American. They were also encouraged and supported by the Soviet Union to be hostile to the United States government and American corporations. Kennedy and his advisers considered Soviet nuclear weapons in Cuba an act of unreasonable aggression, if not an act war, that could not be ignored. Nuclear weapons launched from Cuba could have destroyed every major US city on the East Coast, killing millions of Americans in a matter of minutes.

Every past act of communist aggression, every foreign policy response, every failed diplomatic effort, every incident of global antagonism, even the Bay of Pigs fiasco, became an arsenal of knowledge for Kennedy and his aides in the handling of the Cuban Missile Crisis. Kennedy knew he could not trust his Pentagon. It was in the war business, after all, and he was in the peace business. Still, Kennedy needed to come to some sort of military or diplomatic resolution, and quickly.

In an Oval Office meeting, the Soviet ambassador to the United States unabashedly lied to the president about the presence of nuclear weapons in Cuba. At the United Nations, the Soviets officially continued to deny their involvement of placing nuclear weapons in Cuba, until Kennedy's ambassador exposed the irrefutable photoreconnaissance evidence.

For thirteen days, the administration sat in the catbird's seat. Keeping the hotheaded warmongers at the Pentagon at bay, Commander in Chief Kennedy created EXCOMM, made up of his closest national security advisers and Cabinet members, to find a peaceful yet firm resolution. Kennedy, like FDR and Ike, built up his military arsenal for just such an event.

When Kennedy invited a select group of congressional leaders to the White House to explain the details of the situation, tensions ran high and they attacked Kennedy's slow decision-making prowess. Feeling isolated and betrayed, Kennedy responded, "If they want this job, they can have it."

In the end, cooler heads prevailed and Kennedy imposed an effective naval blockade of Cuba, which the Soviet ships did not violate. Kennedy's "flexible response" diplomacy avoided a nuclear confrontation. A UN approved resolution was crafted that both Khrushchev and Kennedy could live with. The world had come perilously close to a full scale nuclear war. In spite of post-Vienna Summit teletype, the superpowers agreed to advance their communication link by establishing a "Hot Line", a direct and secure telephone connection between the White House and the Kremlin, in an effort to prevent future miscommunications.

The resolution in Cuba did not end Kennedy's concerns with communism. China's advancements in Southeast Asia replaced Kennedy's challenges with the Soviet Union. Laos and Vietnam were feared to be the initial objectives that would create the "domino effect," a political science theorem that communism would spread from one nation to the next, falling like dominos, until all of Southeast Asia was communist, with Australia as the ultimate objective. This theory was beyond reproach, and like Truman and Eisenhower before him Kennedy committed US forces to Vietnam to abate the "Red tide" of communist advancement.

Yet Vietnam was in chaos and rapidly becoming Kennedy's Korea. Similar to Korea, Vietnam was split in two. The Red Chinese supported North Vietnam, and the United States supported the ruling Diem brothers in South Vietnam. In early November 1963, there was a bloody coup and the Diem brothers were assassinated. Kennedy was shaken. He had not ordered the coup, but it had the CIA's fingerprints all over it.

The fall of 1963 was a paradox for the Kennedy administration. Kennedy had effectively signed a Comprehensive Nuclear Test Ban Treaty with the Soviet Union and the United Kingdom in late summer. It was the first of its kind. The treaty called for halting all nuclear test detonations everywhere except underground. Kennedy was exceedingly proud of achieving progress with the Soviets, but now his critics were after him about the Diem assassinations.

Anti-Kennedy forces at home claimed he was "soft on communism" and not doing enough to prevent its encroachment. Had they only been as well informed. Kennedy believed that US foreign policies should not be viewed just as anticommunist, but rather proactive measures that promoted peace and democracy around the world. With all the brushfires burning around the globe, and his impulsive reaction to them, Kennedy was not allowed the opportunity to make his point. He displayed US financial and military strengths as an enticement to smaller and weaker nations to join his strategy of peace, freedom and Democracy, he just needed more time for his objectives to take root.

The Kennedy administration had been quietly using the CIA to oust Castro from power. Kennedy's brother Bobby, the attorney general, who was overseeing this mission, was becoming concerned with the effectiveness of "Operation Mongoose" and wanted the sabotage and assassination plots expedited for the 1964 election. Although the effort was politically intriguing, it could not be mentioned, as it was a covert action.

Politically, Kennedy was uneasy that the Republicans would produce a hardline anticommunist hawk to challenge and defeat him in the 1964 election, and he was correct to be concerned. Kennedy had a string of seven successful elections, and the next year's election would be his last. He was adamant that he was not going to lose it. With all that was going on in his public and private life, with the exception of the Bay of Pigs and Berlin, Kennedy had escaped scandal.

His political operatives, particularly Kenny O'Donnell, were inclined to agree with his reelection assessment and encouraged a southern campaign swing to kick off the 1964 campaign. Kennedy planned to visit Florida, a key southern state with a large Cuban population who deserved his attention after his mishandling of the Bay of Pigs and Castro.

There was also an internal Democratic Party issue in Texas, also a key state for reelection, which required presidential fence mending. So the pre-Thanksgiving Day campaign trip to Florida would also include the vice president's home state of Texas. The first lady—who was pregnant and unable to campaign in 1960 but had now become a political asset due to her global popularity and stylish good looks—agreed to accompany her husband, and the political operatives were delighted.

The first couple traveled to Florida and was well received, as they were on their next stop in Houston, Texas. The following day in Dallas, Kennedy was shot and killed while riding in an open-air convertible. The sniper was a former US Marines sharpshooter, now an avowed communist with Cuban connections, who disregarded the opportunity of a frontal assault and, like a coward, shot Kennedy in the back before blowing his head off.

Kennedy instantly became a Cold War martyr. The nation and the world came to a screeching halt. The assassination was profoundly indescribable. Southern school children cheered that the "nigger lover" president was dead. A great crusade of academic and philosophical excellence had been silenced. Under the Constitution, the transition of power was immediate. Lyndon Baines Johnson was now the president, before the country had a moment to comprehend what had happened.

The Kennedy assassination and the events of the following four days are seared into the national psyche and the minds of all those who are old enough to remember it and the emotional tumult it caused the nation and the world. Even my five-year-old brain vividly recorded the memory so that I can still recall the first time I saw my mother cry.

My father was returning from Washington that Friday. His birthday was the day before, and my mother had planned a party that evening. When he arrived home, he was supposedly met with a multi-page Western Union telegram from the White House detailing the president's funeral plans. It included the president's wish to be buried at Holyhood Cemetery in Brookline and the diplomatic protocol to be followed. It took hours for him to get in touch with the White House and Kenny O'Donnell, who had personally brought the fallen president's body back to Washington. He informed my father to disregard the telegram and return to Washington for the funeral.

My father stayed on as the Northeast director of the SBA. Most of the Irish Mafia and White House staff returned to Boston. We would see them all the time. They moved like dark shadows against a white wall. The Technicolor president whom they all knew and loved was gone, and so was their guiding light. People used to ask Mr. O'Donnell if he thought it was a conspiracy. "Look, no matter what happened, death is final, and any second-guessing will not change the fact that he is dead," was his reply.

I asked my father if he still went to the White House under Johnson. He said he did, but it was not the same, and he quoted an anonymous source: "They still serve champagne at the White House. It just doesn't seem to have as much sparkle any more."

Things changed that day. This event, and the subsequent historic events that followed in JFK's absence, continue to serve as a vivid reminder of the disruptive power of political assassination. Additionally, it serves as the fulcrum of the shift in power away from the pragmatic "classic liberal" to Johnson's progressive style of legislative liberalism. It also benchmarks the highpoint of the Democratic Party in the twentieth century, just fifty years after Woodrow Wilson's inauguration, and our long, slow slide into socialism.

9

LBJ & THE LAST GREAT SOCIETY

"I took an oath. I became President. But for millions of Americans I was still illegitimate, a naked man with no presidential covering, a pretender to the throne, an illegal usurper. And then there was Texas, my home, the home of both the murder and the murderer. And then there were the bigots and the dividers and the Eastern intellectuals, who were waiting to knock me down before I could even begin to stand up. The whole thing was unbearable."[6]

President Johnson, Mrs. Kennedy & Mr. O'Donnell

Courtesy of the Lyndon Baines Johnson Presidential Library and Museum

---

6 Doris Kearns, Lyndon Johnson & the American Dream, New York: Harper & Row, 1976, p. 170.

Johnson was right. Before he could begin his own consti-tutional presidency, he first needed to complete Kennedy's unfinished business. First for consideration was the civil rights legislation that President Kennedy proposed during his nation-ally televised speech of June 11, 1963.

"The heart of the question is whether all Americans are to be afforded equal rights and equal opportunities, whether we are going to treat our fellow Americans as we want to be treated."

Johnson, as caretaker to his predecessor's legacy, combined his expansive legislative skills with emotionally charged Kennedy currency to propose a fully comprehensive and legally enforce-able civil rights legislation package to a somber Congress.

This was not an easy bill to pass. Regardless of the bloody Civil War a hundred years earlier, the nation was still cultur-ally and socially segregated. As a senator, Johnson had strug-gled to pass previous civil rights legislation that neither healed the South nor provided blacks with equal access or economic opportunity.

This new effort would require a consensus of solidarity from the academic, cultural, and political hierarchy to make it purposeful. Eastern intellectuals, black leaders, southern Dixiecrats, and conservative Republicans would all have to agree that the proposed bill was profoundly inclusive and legally viable as well as satisfactory to the Kennedy agenda.

Amazingly, Johnson got it passed. In the end, more Republicans voted for the Civil Rights Acts of 1964 than Democrats. Go figure. This legislation would become the inaugural effort of the Johnson administration to establish itself as a legitimate presidency and create the "Great Society" as an extension of Kennedy's New Frontier.

Johnson knew that the political validity of his programs would be challenged in years to come, but he needed to distance himself from Kennedy's memory and get down to the business of leading the nation. He had given up being Senate majority leader in 1960 to join the Kennedy ticket, and as a result he endured nearly three years as the emasculated baboon of the Kennedy White House.

Despite the events that elevated Johnson to the presidency, it was time for him to stop reacting and start behaving presidential. In an attempt to describe Johnson's Washington of 1964, James Reston of the *New York Times* scribed, "Everything is less romantic and more practical; part regret and part relief; beer instead of champagne; not fancy but plain; and in many ways more natural and hopefully more durable."

Part of this new Washington was validated by Johnson's landslide victory in 1964. He did not just win with the highest populist percentage since 1824; the most liberal Congress since 1936 rode in on his coattails. Democrats gained enough seats to control more than two-thirds of each chamber, a 68–32 majority in the Senate and a 295–140 margin in the House of Representatives. It was a mandate on which he could finally hang his ten-gallon hat; Johnson was our man for the job.

With his new rubber-stamp liberal Congress; Johnson formulated the programs of his Great Society. Of the eighty-seven bills submitted to Congress, Johnson signed eighty-four of them into law. That is 96 percent, arguably the most successfully progressive legislative docket since Wilson.

As with his Democratic predecessors, Johnson expanded consumer protection, including measures involving warning labels on cigarette packaging, motor vehicle safety, child safety, food safety, environmental safety, and truth in lending for credit card companies.

Ideologically, he expanded cultural centers; he created the National Endowments for the Arts and the Public Broadcasting System. Johnson was becoming a Renaissance man.

As a continuation of the Civil Rights Acts of 1964, and marking the beginning of Johnson's presidential mandate, Congress approved the Voting Rights Act of 1965, preventing poll taxes and literacy requirements for blacks at voting stations. A haughty Lyndon Johnson once stated, "I'll have these Niggers voting Democratic for the next 200 years."

As the baby boomers began entering the workforce, Johnson forecast that their additional income matched with his legislative tax breaks would encourage more conspicuous consumer spending, and the additional revenues could fund his progressive budget. He was right for a while, and then he was very wrong.

Similar to the New Deal, Johnson's new budget allowed for a War on Poverty. If passed, it would put the onus of responsibility squarely on the shoulders of the "Community Action" teams, and not on Congress, to manage these new efforts with educational programs and hands-on job training. He called upon Kennedy brother-in-law Sargent Shriver, director of the Peace Corps, as his chief architect for the Great Society.

Shriver was a profoundly compassionate man. His experiences, education, religious faith, and progressive philosophy remain unmatched as a singular intellectual resource for domestic policy. He could speak to Daniel Patrick Moynihan's report on government's role in assisting the economic underclass, especially blacks and their high rate of out-of-wedlock births. He could subjectively discuss the racist media coverage of the black community. He was a realist with idealistic expectations. I knew Mr. Shriver well, as he was the father of my friend Timothy, and I spent countless hours listening to his distinct and inspiring rationale for each of the independent objectives they attained and the obstacles from their critics they needed to overcome. It was a social revolution.

Together, Shriver and Johnson established the Job Corps, Volunteers in Service to America (VISTA, a domestic version of the Peace Corps), Upward Bound, and Head Start, which provided preschool education and nutritional programs for the poor.

Johnson expanded coverage of Social Security, created Medicare for all citizens over sixty years of age, and Medicaid for state administers for those of public assistance. He also increased Aid to Families with Dependent Children (AFDC), otherwise known as welfare.

Critics responded that Johnson was encouraging poor black mothers to have more babies to increase the amount of their weekly welfare checks and to forgo a responsible relationship with the father, who would bear no parental, social, and financial obligation to the child. The criticism was certainly systematic racism, but to the highly educated eastern elite, racism was a footnote to overlook. They believed that one should never deny progressive social reform for the many, based upon the probable, yet still uncertain, bad actions of the few. The welfare state.

The unfortunate reality is that the less educated and less informed mindset of the poor viewed the welfare programs as an opportunity to abuse the system rather than to benefit from it. The confines of the human condition produced an underclass of "welfare mothers" that, despite congressional reform, has continued to expand. In fact, out-of-wedlock births have tripled since the Great Society was implemented. Today, over 40 percent of all US births are to unwed mothers.

It is a fact that unwed birth rates are highest among minorities. For black women it is 72.3 percent, followed by Hispanics at 52.5 percent. Rates for non-Hispanic white and Asian or Pacific Islander women are lower, in the 40 percent range. Most important, 36 percent of all unwed mothers' births are into poverty. As a result, child poverty has become a national epidemic and perpetuates racial bigotry.[7]

The federal government operates over seventy means-tested welfare programs that provide cash, food, housing, medical care, and targeted social services to poor and low-income persons. In fiscal year 2010, federal and state governments spent over $400 billion on means-tested welfare for low-income families with children. Roughly $300 billion went to single-parent families. Through the Medicaid system, taxpayers pay for most nonmarital births and the mother and child will continue to receive some form of welfare assistance for nearly two decades after the child is born. These are unimpressive statics for the remnants of the noble Great Society, and are increasingly abhorrent when mingled with the Immigration and Nationality Act of 1965.

The "wretched refuse" of immigrants prior to 1965 in America hailed predominantly from Western Europe. As most European nationalities have effectively been beating the brains out of each other for centuries, they also have formulated cultural and ethnic identities of sovereign borders, languages, nationalism, and self-worth. When they came to America it was

---

7 National Vital Statistics Reports, 2010.

for opportunity and to leave oppression and starvation behind. They were glad for the opportunity and a fresh start, and they would have swum here if need be.

My maternal pre-famine Irish great-grandfather and his brother sailed to America on their own fishing vessel to earn a living and evade British exploitation. They slept on their boat, as they were not allowed anywhere else to live. The Brahmins of Boston met them with the same racial and religious hatred as the British in Dublin. Check that: the decedents of British pilgrims who sailed to America centuries earlier to escape racial and religious persecution were now inflicting racial and religious persecution, and this was before the masses of starving, infectious, and destitute Irish showed up in the 1840s.

The Irish, like every ethnic group, eventually overcame the bigotry. First they assimilated then they got a job, educated their children, attended their houses of worship, and eventually entered politics. They usually improved their living conditions; they married according to their religion, sometimes across ethnic backgrounds.

When I was a kid, a "mixed marriage" was an Irish father and an Italian mother. The father drank beer and the mother cooked good food. The children attended parochial schools, grew up, and got a job in some form of government, or went to college and ventured into the private sector. America was the land where you could be born poor and die rich, and every immigrant wanted a piece of the American Dream. Yet something is lost when it is not earned or sacrifices are not made. Maybe it's the missing gene of immigrants from places other than Western Europe yearning to breathe free, or maybe it's just standardized fraud.

The Immigration and Nationality Act of 1965 was initially viewed by President Johnson as a philosophical component of his Great Society. Originally proposed by President Kennedy as a civil rights reform initiative, it was effectively lobbied in his memory by his brothers in the US Senate. Yet, the genius of it, I believe, is a brilliantly crafted piece of sub-rosa legislation drafted by social progressives who sought to expand the future Democratic Party voting base by changing the ethnic face of America.

Officially known as the Hart-Celler Act, it transformed the federal immigration policy of a "quota system" for a specific number of Western European nations into a policy acknowledging immigrants' occupations or labor skills and their family relationships with US citizens or residents. It also expanded geographical horizons to include recently decolonized nations in Asia, Africa, Latin America, and the Caribbean islands as an alternative to creeping communist forces.

When passed, annual visa quotas were restricted at 170,000 for each nation, which did not include immediate relatives of US citizens or "special immigrants," otherwise known as refugees or asylum seekers. Think Cuban exiles.

President Johnson dramatically signed it into law at the base of the Statue of Liberty on October 3, 1965.

"This bill that we will sign today is not a revolutionary bill," he said. "It does not affect the lives of millions. It will not reshape the structure of our daily lives or add importantly to either our wealth or our power."

Like hell this bill did not affect the lives of millions of Americans. No prior form of legislation has influenced the cultural and ethnic fabric of the nation more than Hart-Celler. The act has reshaped the very structure of our daily lives and has diminished both our national economic wealth and our nationalist integrity. "Ethnics" are now politicized by campaigns, and as such most people use hyphenated designations to describe their cultural backgrounds. That's not revolutionary?

President Kennedy's original proposal made "skills-based" immigration the priority, yet the thrust of the act has become the "family reunification" component. As national quotas are exempt from this designation, it has become the source of abuse and the antithesis of Kennedy's original intent. According to noted historian Otis Graham, "Family reunification puts the decision of who comes to America in the hands of foreigners. Those decisions are out of the hand of the Congress—they just set up a formula and its kinship. Frankly, it could be called nepotism."

The Civil Rights Acts of 1964 and 1965 were not enough for Kennedy's brothers, Bobby and Teddy, now both serving in the US Senate. They wanted to perpetuate JFK's legacy with a different version of his intended recalibration.

A sentimental Teddy Kennedy assured his fellow senators that "our cities will not be flooded with a million immigrants annually. It will not upset the ethnic mix of our society. It will not relax the standards of admission."

Time has proven him categorically incorrect. After a thirty-year experiment with open borders, whites no longer constitute a majority of Californians or residents of New York City. Prior to the 1965 reform, immigration was roughly three hundred thousand per year. Today it exceeds one million. The population of legal immigrants has grown from 3.3 million in 1965 to over thirty-six million, with an additional twelve million undocumented aliens living in the United States. Yep, that is nearly fifty million foreign-born people living in the United States, and nearly half of them live in poverty and on federal welfare.

In 1965 Senator Robert Kennedy predicted a total of five thousand immigrants from India; actual numbers exceeded his estimates by one thousand times. He also promised that, "Immigration from any single country would be limited to 10 percent of the total." Yet Hispanics have made up nearly 50 percent of all immigrants since 1968, and 20 percent have come from Mexico alone.

The Kennedys were not alone. Senator Hiram Fong calculated that "the people from [Asia] will never reach 1 percent of the population." Asians currently account for 3 percent of the population and will swell to near 10 percent by 2050 if present trends continue. There are over 1.3 billion people living in China alone.

The bill's cosponsor, Representative Emanuel Celler of New York, insisted, "There will not be, comparatively speaking, many Asians or Africans entering this country." Today, the number of Asians and Africans entering this country each year exceeds the annual average of three hundred thousand during the 1960s.

There were opponents to this act, such as Republican Congressman William Miller of New York, whose predictions have proved eerily accurate. "We estimate that if the president gets his way, and the current immigration laws are repealed, the number of immigrants next year will increase threefold and in subsequent years will increase even more," he was quoted as saying in the *New York Times* on September 8, 1964. "Shall we, instead, look at this situation realistically and begin solving our own unemployment problems before we start tackling the world's?"

Here are Teddy Kennedy's justifications during a National Public Radio interview in May 2006:

NPR: But the level of even legal immigration has increased dramatically since 1965, even though many supporters of the legislation then said it would not.

KENNEDY: Everybody obviously wants to come, because this is the land of opportunity, but we've seen a rather dramatic shift as well in terms of the birthrate here. That was not really foreseen.

NPR: What's striking about the debate in 1965 is how so many people did not expect a huge increase in immigration, or a change in the demographics of the nation. You told Congress that immigration levels would remain "substantially the same," and that "the ethnic mix of this country will not be upset." Why weren't these changes foreseen?

KENNEDY: There were enormous changes as a result of illegal immigration. A lot of the antagonism, frustration, and anger is better focused at the illegality and the illegals that came here in very significant numbers. [People] are certainly frustrated by the illegality and the explosion of illegals who come here that have impact in terms of the economy, depressing wages, and taking jobs.

Really? Birthrates? Illegal Immigration? Thirty-six million people living in America who were not born here, ten times the amount in 1965, and you are justifying the economic consequences with illegal aliens? What happened to the quota of maximum visas of 170,000 per year?

How could Johnson have gotten it so wrong? How could we have let him get away with it? Was he bullied and threatened by the errant Knights of Camelot? Was he an ideological dolt, or just hopelessly naive? Regardless, the passage of this act, commingled with the entitlements of his Great Society, has produced the greatest financial burden and broad-based ethnical dilemma in the nation's history.

It was one thing to elevate millions of Americans from poverty and give them a chance to fulfill their American dream. It is an entirely different objective to direct the benefits created for naturalized citizens to strangers who have not worked or earned the right to such benefits. For Congress to propose and Johnson to sign such a bill without factual and detailed data is reprehensible. The long-term economic impact on the nation's resources is not only fiscally irresponsible, but it is systematically offensive to the workers whose wages are used to pay for these programs.

According to the US Census Bureau, in 2008 and 2009, 2.4 million new immigrants (legal and illegal) settled in the United States, even though 8.2 million jobs were lost over the same period. There were 14.5 million immigrants and their US-born children (under 18) who lacked health insurance. They accounted for 31.9 percent of the entire uninsured population. Immigrants and their children were 16.8 percent of the nation's total population.

This act will go down in the annals of American history as either one of the greatest frauds ever perpetuated against US taxpayers or one of the greatest financial miscalculations in the history of the world. One thing is for sure: There is no way to rewind the clock, and under current circumstances, there is no hope or realistic attempt to halt the influx of foreigners, legally or illegally, onto our soil. It was predicted that for the first time, in 2012 the Hispanic vote would determine the outcome of the general election.

Recently a friend of mine, a retired US Marine, was required to visit his local Social Security office to address his benefits while he undergoes chemotherapy treatments for cancer. He could not believe what he witnessed. "I thought that Social Security was established to aid the worker, but to my surprise, I was the only white guy in the room and the only one speaking English."

Being a former SSI/Medicaid caseworker, I asked him how he knew that they were not former workers. "Really, you tell me where a dozen of eighty-year-old Asian women, who could not speak English, worked legally and paid into Social Security. And who was the twenty-year-old kid who drove them there in his van?" I was speechless, and this was only one Social Security office outside Boston.

In 2010, total income for Social Security was $781.1 billion, and expenditures were $712.5 billion, which meant a total net increase in assets of $68.6 billion. Assets in 2010 were $2.6 trillion, an amount that is expected to be adequate to cover the next ten years. In 2023, total income and interest earned on assets are projected to no longer cover expenditures for Social Security. The trust fund would then be exhausted by 2036 without immediate legislative action.

When I was fatherless during my college years, President Reagan cut my Social Security benefits during the summer months to help balance the budget. I agreed. Why pay me when I could go out and get a summer job? Now the nation is $16 trillion in debt while immigration swindlers pass out fliers in China explaining federal benefits to potential emigrants, how to get into the United States, how to bring your family, and how to live off government entitlement programs in perpetuity.

Whatever happened to "America is a nation where you can be born poor and die rich"? Or whatever happened to "charity begins at home"? Yeah, whatever.

10

VIETNAM, VIOLENCE, & VITRIOL

The other bit of Kennedy's unfinished business for Johnson was America's military involvement in Vietnam. Johnson handled it poorly, and this engagement became the most disastrous US foreign policy exercise of the twentieth century, as well as the beginning of the end for the once-powerful and popular Democratic Party. It remains the dark cloud of his presidency, burnt into the memory of the baby boomer generation.

Vietnam was a colony of French Indochina in the mid-nineteenth century. As the indigenous Vietnamese were less than pleased by being occupied by the French, there were constant clashes. During WWII, Vietnam fell to invading Japanese forces. In the aftermath of WWII, the French returned to Vietnam—again, much to the displeasure of the Vietnamese people and their new communist leader, Ho Chi Minh. Seeking autonomy and independence, Ho Chi Minh and his followers promptly went to war with France. This is known as the First French Indochina War. After five years of fighting, the 1954 Geneva Accords established a divided Vietnam. The North was controlled by Ho Chi Minh, the South by prewar, pro-French Emperor Bao Dai.

The dissatisfied South Vietnamese Prime Minister Ngo Dinh Diem quickly deposed the emperor and founded the Republic of (South) Vietnam. As Diem was faulted for being out of touch with his people—too French and too Catholic for the nationalistic and Buddhist Vietnamese—he refused to hold open elections as stipulated in the Geneva Accords. Fearing overwhelming communist proliferation, the US government concurred, and so began the Second French Indochina War and thus US involvement in Vietnam. The United States had just negotiated the resolution of the Korean conflict, and here we were again, in divided Vietnam. Great idea: get out of one divisive Asian conflict and get into a second.

Kennedy had inherited this anticommunist "containment" mess from both Truman and Eisenhower, and he remained adamant not to get pulled into another land war in Asia as we had in Korea. Yet, as North Vietnamese forces began heading south, the United States was required to address its foreign policy response to the "red spread." As such, the United States began defending lines of demarcation and engaging in military maneuvers against the well-armed North Vietnamese guerilla forces.

The departing Eisenhower had warned Kennedy of the Vietnam quagmire. Yet, after the embarrassment of the Bay of Pigs, the Berlin Wall, and the unilateral negotiation with the communists on Laos, Kennedy did not want to lose a fourth straight foreign policy initiative and dug his heels on the communist brushfire burning in Vietnam—sort of.

Kennedy formed the antiguerilla Green Berets and ordered sixteen thousand military personnel into Vietnam, up from the previous nine hundred "advisers." John Kenneth Galbraith, Kennedy's friend and foreign emissary, also warned of the "danger we shall replace the French as a colonial force in the area and bleed as the French did."

The US-backed Prime Minister Diem and his brother were assassinated in a bloody coup in early November 1963. Kennedy was shaken. The Department of Defense supported Diem, but the State Department did not. Kennedy's ambassador to Vietnam, Henry Cabot Lodge Jr., his former political opponent, held a party for the coup's leaders at the American compound, telling the president, "The prospects now are for a shorter war."

Just a few weeks later, Kennedy, like Diem, was assassinated, and the putrid baton of US military involvement in Vietnam was passed on to Johnson. Two days after Kennedy's death, the new president said to a small group, "We should stop playing cops and robbers [a reference to Diem's failed leadership] and get back to...winning the war...Tell the generals in Saigon that Lyndon Johnson intends to stand by our word...[to] win the contest against the externally directed and supported communist conspiracy."

Two days after that, Johnson reversed Kennedy's official disengagement policy to withdraw US troops from Vietnam and expanded our commitment to the new South Vietnamese government. Johnson, as it turned out, was more interested in establishing the Great Society as his presidential legacy than handling the Vietnam issue, and he allowed the Pentagon to do his thinking for him. A massive miscalculation. One thing Kennedy learned during the Cuban issues was not to trust the Pentagon, which was run by warmongers who were happy only when in battle.

In August 1964, the *USS Maddox*, a destroyer patrolling Vietnam's Gulf of Tonkin, responded to three antagonistic North Vietnamese torpedo boats with gunfire. It was a trumped-up event, but in the end four North Vietnamese sailors were killed. It was the incident that Johnson required to view as an act of war. He lobbied Congress for the Gulf of Tonkin Resolution, giving him the power to go to war. What a disaster. The Gulf of Tonkin Incident "is an oft-cited example of the way in which Johnson misled the American people to gain support for his foreign policy in Vietnam."[8]

The information we have today verifies what most Americans came to believe: that the secretary of defense, his generals, and the Pentagon all knew by 1966 that the United States could not win the war in Vietnam. Yet Pentagon bravado is epitomized by

---

8 Louise Gerdes (Ed.), Examining Issues through Political Cartoons: The Vietnam War, Madison, WI: Greenhaven Press, 2005, p. 25.

Air Force General Curtis Lemay's promise to "bomb them (the North Vietnamese) back to the Stone Age."

The battles continued for years; more troops committed, more causalities. The Vietnamese knew they could not be beaten. North Vietnam Prime Minister Pham Van Dong said during an interview with *New York Times* reporter Harrison E. Salisbury, "And how long do you Americans want to fight... one year? Two years? Three years? Five years, Ten years? Twenty years? We will be glad to accommodate you."[9]

In early 1968, a demoralized Johnson authorized a mutually agreed upon cease-fire in observance of Tet, the Vietnamese New Year celebration. The North Vietnamese broke the cease-fire and attacked the major cities and targets in the South, including the US Embassy in Saigon. The Tet Offensive became the most revealing event of the war and epitomized the reality that the US forces were not winning. Similar to Korea, the United States was destined for an impasse. Broadcast journalist Walter Cronkite reported after Tet, "For it seems now more certain than ever that the bloody experience of Vietnam is to end in a stalemate...But it is increasingly clear to this reporter that the only rational way out then will be to negotiate, not as victors, but as an honorable people who lived up to their pledge to defend democracy, and did the best they could."

---

9 David Halbertstam, The Best & the Brightest, New York: Random House, 1969, p. 665.

Johnson was dismayed. "If I've lost Cronkite, I've lost Middle America."

By 1968 Johnson had 550,000 troops inside Vietnam and was losing one thousand soldiers a week. Johnson was suffering from a "credibility gap". The American people had grown doubtful of our involvement in Vietnam, and a majority believed the war to be militarily and morally unsound and supported withdrawal.

Johnson's fellow Democrats echoed these views on the Senate floor. In the fall of 1967, Eugene McCarthy declared he was running for president in opposition to Johnson's wartime policies. George McGovern warned of the beginning of World War III. Bobby Kennedy misquoted Roman Historian Tacitus: "We (they) made a desert and we called it peace." Senator Thurston B. Morton from Kentucky stated Johnson was "brainwashed by the military industrial complex." In the fall of 1968, even Vice President Hubert Humphrey opposed the war.

As Lyndon Johnson explained to Doris Kearns, "I knew from the start that I was bound to be crucified either way I moved. If I left the woman I really loved, the Great Society, in order to get involved in that bitch of a war on the other side of the world, then I would lose everything at home. All my programs...But if I left the war and let the communists take over South Vietnam, then I would be seen as a coward and my nation would be seen as an appeaser, and we would both find it impossible to accomplish anything for anybody anywhere on the entire globe."

There were nearly seven million college kids in America and half were terrified they might be conscripted and sent to Vietnam. They took over their campuses, burned their draft cards, and chanted, "Hey, Hey, LBJ, how many kids did you kill today?" In the beginning Johnson agreed and stated, "We don't want our American boys to do the fighting for Asian boys." He should have taken his own advice.

Every night when Americans turned on their new color television sets, the *Huntley-Brinkley Report* gave a daily tally of those killed in action, missing in action, and wounded. Grim Technicolor footage of American teenagers, covered in blood, missing appendages, and shrieking in pain was the news of the day, every day and every night. It was insufferable. War had entered into America's living rooms, and parents hated it and blamed Johnson. My brother, with a crew cut, a badge, a young wife, and son, would just look at my father as if to say, "What the hell is going on?" My father would shut off the television, make himself a drink, and find a new perch far away from the television and the harsh reality of his party's foreign policy.

On Sunday evenings, the *Smothers Brothers Comedy Hour* and *Laugh-In*, along with every other comedy show that aired during the rest of the week, mocked Johnson and the war. Proud veterans couldn't tolerate it. They had never spoken of what they saw or did in war, and now the entire nation was turning on them, their sons, and their commander in chief. During one Sunday night family dinner, one of my brothers, fearful of being drafted, referred to Johnson as a "cow" and a war criminal. I don't know if it were the length of his hair, his bell-bottoms, or the fact that my father knew he was right, but my father flipped out and pounded the table, stating he would not hear of it, criticizing his president, his country, his party. He worked for the president of the United States, after all, and any such talk was treasonous.

This same scene was being played out in every living room and dining room and on every college campus across the country. America was a nation divided and on the decline. The war was killing us, figuratively at home and literally overseas. Guess who was appearing on the political horizon? Tricky Dick Nixon, looking to make a repeat performance in presidential politics.

The telephone in my father's den rang constantly. Either the war had to end or Johnson had to go, but who would replace him?

Produced by Posters, Inc. Holyoke, MA www.postersinc.com

11

BOBBY KENNEDY'S CAMPAIGN

There was no question that the Kennedy loyalists disliked Johnson. It began during the primary season in 1960. It followed through to the convention, on the campaign trail, and even into the White House. Johnson's infantile outbursts were symptoms of greater character flaws, and the Kennedy administration had no patience for his childish behavior. Yet it was the event in Dallas, the one that made Johnson president, which became the watershed moment when Kennedy's staff began to despise him.

Moments after taking the oath of office on Air Force One, Johnson patronized Kennedy's grieving staff. "I need you more now than he ever needed you," he told them. At first these untimely requests for loyalty smacked of insincerity. But after the staff collectively determined that Johnson had regurgitated the exact same line to each and every one of them, he was perceived as an abhorrent pile of warm Texas bullshit.

Johnson was known as a crude dude, calling aides into the presidential bathroom while sitting on the crapper. Bobby Kennedy thought his brother a gentleman and Johnson an animal, and he was right. Albeit that LBJ was everything JFK was not, he was everything that Bobby Kennedy wanted to be—and that was president. The crucial question for Bobby was how was he going to take the presidency away from Johnson without splitting the party?

There was a "Good Bobby" and a "Bad Bobby," and each expected undying loyalty and unambiguous respect from his staff, and both got it. Bobby Kennedy accepted the fact that a few of JFK's White House staff members remained with the Johnson administration, and he did not begrudge them; they worked for the president, after all. Bobby remained reasonably certain those staffers would jump ship at the first guarantee of his presidential bid. For by attaining the presidency, Bobby would become the redeemer of the true realm, sitting aloft on his brother's throne, reconvening his court. Real medieval stuff, strictly Arthurian, if one is a believer in the concept of Camelot.

But this was twentieth-century America, and the Twenty-fifth Amendment of the Constitution had recently been fine-tuned on the subject of whom was president—and that was Johnson. Democrats, whether former Cabinet members or currently disgruntled members of Congress, would support the leader of the party. No Democrat walks out on a sitting president. Never. Former Kennedy White House staff members and the big-city bosses all agreed, first and foremost, on loyalty to the president.

Yet this president, as commander in chief, the presumed mastermind of the Vietnam War, was dividing the Senate into warmongering hawks on one side of the aisle and peace-seeking doves on the other. It was becoming clear to all that this president had lied to the country not only about the realities of this terrible war, but also about the prospects of winning it. Democrat operatives were pleading with Bobby to run for president and unify the party, yet Kennedy was cautious of the risk. Quite a conundrum, but hey, man, it was the sixties.

The 1960s had become a decade not of peace, as JFK had hoped, but of violence and division. There were endless civil rights incidents in the South. There were race riots, some fatal. The president had been assassinated and his killer shot to death on live television. There were inner cities burning and hatred all across the nation. The police response was out of control; water cannons, attack dogs, and billy clubs were mercilessly used on citizens. The bloody faces of American citizens, mostly black, joined the newsreels of bloody American soldiers, mostly black, on the evening news. As former attorney general, the highest legal seat in the land, Bobby Kennedy thought that what was happening to our culture was both illegal and unjust. The Great Society wasn't working. People were pissed off and becoming violent, and Bobby Kennedy was now stymied in the Senate. There was little he could do about the events consuming the nation.

His brother Teddy frequently advised him that the Senate was a genteel institution not designed for individual conquests. In the rarefied Senate there remained a proper protocol, a pecking order of committees and subcommittees, and finally compromise and a bill. The executive orders are housed at the other end of Pennsylvania Avenue.

Bobby Kennedy was too impatient and too decisive for the Senate. He would complain that citizens from someplace in New York would write him about a local park or something similar. He did not want to work on those constituency issues. He wanted to lead, he wanted civil rights, he wanted to end poverty, and he wanted to stop the war. He was full of hellfire yet frozen in the glacial Senate. Fire and ice—never a good mix.

By 1967 Kennedy was persistently annoyed with the lack of effort to end the war. Democratic doves were perched in the Senate, looking for a coalition. In the fall, Eugene McCarthy decided to run against the sitting president because of his Vietnam policy. Bobby Kennedy wanted to lead the skein of doves, but he was forced by party protocol to sit back and observe.

After McCarthy announced, some Kennedy loyalists joined his campaign, feeling as Kennedy did—that anybody but Johnson could end the war. Kennedy's ambitious Senate staff was prodding him, and his wife was nagging him. She wanted him back in the White House, right where she thought her family belonged.

And then there were those who did not, for a myriad of reasons. There was loyalty to the president and the party; fear of splitting the party; and the self-effacing possibility of losing the damn election. There were also safety concerns. Teddy was against it, and Jackie was against it, sagaciously noting that there were people who disliked Jack, and look what happened to him, but people really hated Bobby, and what then was to be expected?

The press would be against him. They had not been kind to Bobby Kennedy, but in reality Bobby Kennedy was not always kind to them. For years the press had portrayed him as a ruthless son of a bitch. It was well known by the press that as Jack's campaign manager, he didn't care what people thought of him but only what voters thought of his brother. He was good at politics but not so great at being a politician.

Bobby Kennedy had been portrayed by the press in New York as a "carpetbagger", an opportunist who ran on his famous name and used the Senate seat as merely a stepping-stone to get back at Johnson and back into the White House. A presidential campaign would play right into their hands. Embittered and biased with envy, the press claimed that presidential power is something fought for, not given. It could get ugly.

McCarthy's primary campaign in New Hampshire had "violet-eyed Smith damsels pinning McCarthy buttons on tattooed millworkers."[10] After Tet, the political storm clouds began to

10   Mary McGrory of the Washington Star as found in Theodore H. White, The Making of the President 1968, New York: Athenaeum Publishers, 1969, p. 99.

rumble, for everything about Vietnam lacked sincerity and credibility. Bobby Kennedy attempted to give Johnson a way out. Bobby asked Johnson to form a Vietnam Commission to conclude that the institution of foreign policy had failed and not the commander in chief. With a scapegoat, Johnson would save face and begin to bring the troops home. But Johnson balked. When Kennedy spoke out against the Vietnam policy, some Democrats branded him a traitor. It was a hopeless scenario.

Bobby Kennedy wrote an article in the *New York Times* about our national dilemma, about "the malaise of the spirit in America" and the failure of material abundance to bring spiritual happiness. "We seek to recapture our country...And that is what the 1968 elections must really be about."

McCarthy nearly tied Johnson in the New Hampshire Democratic primary. New Hampshire was the state with the fewest sons killed in Vietnam, a union-friendly state with virtually no unemployment, and the sitting president got barely half the votes. Johnson sent a political operative to preprimary Wisconsin, and the news was even worse.

Kennedy anguished. He was running out of time, and McCarthy, a man he did not much admire, was taking control of the party. Kennedy would assemble a New York cabal to formulate the decision on whether to run or not to run. The group would cover all the pros and cons, all the dimensions and ramifications of the decision, but it could never reach a consensus. This process would play itself out over and over without resolution. It came to the reality that you are either pregnant or you are not—you are either in or you are out.

These were hard-knuckled, big-city politicians; family members; decisive diplomats; war-worn veterans; and labor leaders—not the types who would easily stand down. They really did want Bobby to run, but they could not solve the Democratic loyalty dilemma. So without a razor-sharp mandate, Bobby was out.

Kennedy would return to Washington and meet with a more enthusiastic group who promised their support, and he was back in. He would call another meeting that evening, where participants would disagree with this thinking, and he was back out. Some nights he would go to bed getting ready to announce his candidacy the next day, only to awake in the morning and renege. He was way too conflicted and asked everyone he came in touch with "Should I run?" and then "Why should I run?"

Kennedy and his band of political comrades finally committed to run for president, yet the only way to run was not to be seen as the Bad Bobby, the ruthless and entitled usurper of the Democratic Party, the heir apparent to his brother's presidency, but as the Good Bobby who entered the race not as an opponent of the sitting commander in chief but as an opponent only to his war with the sole objective of ending it. He was in.

On these Sunday nights when the television shows made a mockery of contemporary America, the private telephone in my father's den would ring all evening. Businessmen, politicians, contributors, advance men, and even nosy neighbors would call to inquire: What was the news? Was Bobby Kennedy in or was he out? My father brushed them away. How could tell them something he didn't know, and then they would press him about McCarthy or Johnson. Political opportunists are always afraid to back the wrong horse and be forced to change horses in midstream, which is political suicide.

"Stick with the ticket" was all he would say in the end.

At the conclusion of each phone call, first my mother would slink in, the kids soon to follow. I listened in on the other extension in his bedroom. "Who was that? Was that the call? What did he say?" It was as if the jury was deadlocked in a life-or-death deliberation. There would be waiting, then a signal flare, then nothing. Finally on a Friday night, he got the call from Kenny O'Donnell: Bobby Kennedy was in and announcing in the morning. My father had received the same call before, to no avail. He took an "I'll believe it when I see it" approach. Bobby Kennedy would speak of the ripples of hope regarding injustice, but he was now emitting ripples of hope out to local Democrats in the political hinterlands of America.

The following morning, the house telephone rang, not the one in the den. "Turn on your television set." It was a rainy and cold Saint Patrick's Day weekend. Bobby Kennedy used the same words, at the same venue as his brother did when he announced his candidacy eight years earlier. Bobby added to his brother's announcement, "I do not run for the presidency merely to oppose any man but to propose new policies. I run because I am convinced that this country is on a perilous course and because I have such strong feelings about what must be done, and I feel that I'm obliged to do all that I can...I do not lightly dismiss the dangers and the difficulties of challenging an incumbent president. But these are not ordinary times, and this is not an ordinary election." Ah, the Good Bobby.

The Bobby Kennedy campaign for president was going to need to act fast. Organization would be most critical. Headquarters and local offices needed to be opened, staff would be required. Mr. O'Donnell moved from Boston to New York. To activate loyalty, state committees were contacted. If already committed to McCarthy, they had a chance to join the winning team without questions of loyalty. This was a different group than the 1960 squad, yet telegrams and letters of support rained in from Jack's old supporters.

The Senate staff needed to be recalibrated from policy to politics. It was the middle of primary season, and there were many voters to meet and speeches to make. They were going to need speechwriters. They got the guys from Jack's group, the ones who actually got it: Richard Goodwin, Arthur Schlesinger, etc.—those guys. The campaign quickly became presidential. As the train burst out of the station and began to pick up speed, the press was starting to follow suit. This was the Bobby

Kennedy campaign. He was no longer the torchbearer, and he had become his own man.

Two weeks later the Kennedy campaign and the nation were delivered a seismic shock: Johnson took himself out of the race for reelection. Kenny O'Donnell predicted it, calling Johnson a "bully and a coward," afraid to go up against Bobby. Chicago Mayor Richard Daley told Bobby Kennedy that Johnson should have "cashed his chips in" long ago. So if Daley were on board, the rest would be history. But first Kennedy needed delegates.

LBJ used a Texan's metaphor in describing his dilemma as two stampeding bulls—the war and the failing economy—coming at him from opposing sides and steering him toward a menacing cliff. "I was being forced to the edge by rioting blacks, demonstrating students, marching welfare mothers, squawking professors, and hysterical reporters. And then the final straw. The thing I feared from the first day of my presidency was actually coming true. Robert Kennedy had openly announced his intentions to reclaim the throne in memory of his brother and the American people, swayed by the magic of the name, were dancing in the streets." [11]Ya gotta laugh, the poor bastard.

Next the Kennedy campaign would have to decimate McCarthy's popularity. Kennedy's prior relationship with McCarthy was tepid at best, and his entering the race after New Hampshire didn't warm it. Bobby asked Teddy to do his

11 Doris Kearns, p.343

dirty work and tell McCarthy what his plans were, but Teddy declined out of professional courtesy.

Bobby Kennedy attacked Eugene McCarthy for being a dove and nothing else. By establishing him as a one-trick pony, Kennedy systematically removed him from any meaningful debate of the many social issues that were plaguing the nation. This was political genius.

The press backlash that Kennedy feared so much became a nonevent. There were still Bobby Kennedy haters and anti-imperialist presidency cynics in the press, but their acerbic delivery read more judgmental than objective. When Kennedy went into the ghettos, sometimes without police protection, he was well received, and the press reported favorably on the aberration. When Kennedy connected to the anger and bitterness of the inner city, the people who appeared truly upset and unstable seemed less so after he left. The Kennedy speech to a group of blacks in Indianapolis that announced the murder of Martin Luther King Jr. was Homeric.

The initial instinct of the crowd was riotous. Kennedy cooled them down. He promised compassion and justice. He spoke of his own brother being shot and killed by a white man. As a result, Indianapolis did not burn that night, while every other major US city did. The press began covering Kennedy as a prism of light.

When Kennedy met with revolutionary black militants, they referred to him as the establishment and embarrassed him with shocking and derogatory remarks. They called Kennedy's black apologizers Uncle Toms. Yet Kennedy took it and listened to them; no other white man ever came to listen. Kennedy did not blame them. They were right—they were voiceless and justifiably angry. So would any US citizen be who could not stand up and be respected as a man. He agreed with them, and together they found simpatico.

"Kennedy's white, but he's all right." Was a campaign slogan.

Kennedy's delivery to the white middle class was confrontational. He promised peace and continued national security, but he asked them if they were aware that in bountiful America children were hungry? Kennedy continued to win primaries, but then came Oregon, where he lost his first one. Not enough pissed off minorities in Oregon.

Kennedy moved on to the California primary. Now, if ever there was a state for Bobby Kennedy to win, it was California. It had it all: Northern California, Southern California, hippies, yippies, and druggies. It had big business, Ronald Reagan as governor, flower power, nuclear power, raisins, grapes and fasting migrant workers who harvested them. It had disenfranchised Native Americans and Latinos. It had big cities—Sacramento, San Francisco, Oakland, Los Angeles, and San Diego—and each was fraught with poverty, unemployment, and prejudice. As I stated, the kaleidoscope of California had it all for Bobby Kennedy's campaign victory.

California also had a fistful of electoral votes, just as many as Kennedy's home state of New York. In 1968, he would have to win either to be elected president. This was it, the big contest, the whole enchilada.

Bobby Kennedy went into California, and the people ripped the clothes right off him. He had rock-star status. They scratched his face, and they pulled his hair. His aides were nervous about the crowds, not just their electricity but also the agitation within them. Kennedy ignored his staff's concerns. He explained that the press was always reporting how so many people hated Bobby Kennedy. Why not let them report about how many people loved him? Bobby Kennedy wasn't ruthless— he was fearless.

Frank Stockton wrote a short story, *The Lady or the Tiger*, basically about how a socially progressive monarch would administer legal justice by allowing the accused the option of choosing between two doors. If the alleged were righteous, he would meet a beautiful lady and marry her. But if guilty, he would meet a hungry tiger that would immediately consume him.

This was a story I was reading in school when Bobby Kennedy was campaigning in California. He won the Democratic primary, of course, and most likely would have been an amazing president, but with apologies to Theodore White's analogy, Bobby Kennedy chose the wrong door when exiting the victory reception, and he was devoured. His poor wife had to watch it all, ecstasy to agony in five minutes, from triumph to tragedy, just like Jack.

As with his President Kennedy, the nation lost a lot when Bobby Kennedy was killed. A lot of promise, a lot of hope, a lot of laughs. Once again a coward, this time an anti-Israeli, a Palestinian immigrant, stole Bobby Kennedy's life with a pistol, a crappy little Saturday night special. How can so much evil come out of something so insignificant and destroy so much good?

That was the end of Bobby Kennedy, dead at forty-two years of age, the father of eleven kids, uncle to dozens more, and the son of two elderly, politically powerful Irish Catholic parents from Boston. This was the third son they had lost violently in the pursuit of his American Dream. *Arragh*, to be Irish is to know that in the end, the world will always break yer heart.

It was tough on the home front. I was kept home from school. It took a day for life to leave Bobby Kennedy's body, and the world grieved that this could happen twice in America. It was the return of so much emotion that had been shut away for five years. Apparently the last man Bobby Kennedy spoke with was Mr. O'Donnell, stating he finally felt he was outside Jack's shadow.

Kenny O'Donnell led his old Harvard football squad into Saint Patrick's Catholic Church in New York City and on the funeral train ride to Washington. Uncle Jim said it was the saddest thing to witness, for now it had happened not just twice to the Kennedys, but twice to Kenny, and Bobby being his best friend. "What marvelous crowds!" [12]noted historian Arthur Schlesinger Jr. to Mr. O'Donnell on the funeral train. Kenny responded, "Yes, but what are they good for?"

I asked my father why he didn't go to Bobby Kennedy's funeral. I know he had a better relationship with Jack, but he knew Bobby well. He said he wasn't invited. His name was on the list in *Esquire* magazine, but I don't think he wanted to go and chose to just ignore it. Soon after, I sat outside with him as he smoked a Lucky Strike, asking him about all this historic stuff that seemed to be swirling around him. Staring at the night sky, "Another one for the ages" was all he said. That was it.

I knew the Irish Mafia would be returning to Boston, this time after only six weeks instead of six years. And I knew they were going to be really down now. But the convention still had to happen, the general election remained a reality, and the Democrats needed a nominee. The den telephone started ringing about a week later.

---

12 Arthur M. Schlesinger Jr., Robert Kennedy and His Times, Boston: Houghton Mifflin Co., 1968, p. 915.

12

THE CHICAGO CONVENTION

"How is it possible that all these people could be so ungrateful to me after I had given them so much? Take the Negroes. I fought for them from the first day I came into office. I spilled my guts out in getting in the Civil Rights Act of 1964 through Congress. I put everything I had into that speech before joint session 1965. I tried to make it possible for every child of every color to grow up in a nice house, to eat a solid breakfast, to attend a decent school, and to get a good and lasting job. I asked so little in return. Just a little thanks. Just a little appreciation. That's all. But look what I get instead. Riots in 175 cities. Looting. Burning. Shooting. It ruined everything. Then take the students. I wanted to help them, too. I fought on their behalf for scholarships and loans and grants. I fought for better teachers and better schools. And look what I got back. Young people by the thousands leaving their universities, marching in the streets, chanting that horrible song about how many kids I killed that day. And the poor, they, too turned on me. When Congress cut the funds for Great Society, they made me Mr. Villain. I remember once going to visit a poor family in Appalachia. They had seven children, all skinny and sick. I promised the mother and father I would make things better for them. I told them all my hopes for their future. They seemed real happy to talk with me, and I felt good about that. But then as I walked toward the door, I noticed two pictures on the shabby wall, one was Jesus Christ on the cross; the other John Kennedy. I felt as if I'd been slapped in the face."[13]

Unlike Kennedy, Johnson was not a man of his time. The reality for Johnson was he should have stayed in the Senate. "He never understood the difference between the Hill and the White House," [14] stated John Roche, a White House aide.

Johnson came into office under dark clouds, and his presidency rapidly became a tropical storm. His heart was in the right place, but his domestic policies were failing and running out of funds. His foreign policy was an unmitigated disaster, and now fellow Democrats was chasing him from office. He planned to retreat to Texas, where he might find a semblance of respect and honor, but before he left Washington, he needed to pass the toxic baton of his party, but to whom? As the long hot summer in Washington wore on, Johnson's behavior became more erratic and problematic. He also began the Paris Peace Talks with the North Vietnamese.

Politically, the Democratic Party was a fractured dream with no heir apparent to restore it. Recent campaign allegiances

---

13 Doris Kearns, p. 340-1.
14 Theodore H. White, p.115

remained mercurial at best. The party needed unity, and Johnson wasn't helping. As usual he was making matters worse.

Bobby Kennedy maintained the majority of the delegate count, now held in abeyance. George McGovern announced his candidacy to provide a home for Kennedy's delegates, a noble gesture, but pure window dressing that quickly vaporized. Eugene McCarthy still maintained an impressive number of delegates, but he openly admitted his doubts of ever being elected president. Johnson was promoting Vice President Hubert Humphrey, maneuvering to keep Teddy Kennedy in mourning on Cape Cod and off the ticket, and all the while playing cat and mouse with Humphrey about the Paris Peace Talks and whether or not he might just reassess his decision not to run and ride into Chicago on a Texan stallion to save the day. Johnson had become such a liability that even his Secret Service detail recommended he not attend the convention, as they could not guarantee his safety. What a wonderful world.

Chicago was also having a long hot summer. When the delegates arrived in late August, they found a city in chaos. Taxicab drivers were on strike, bus drivers were on strike, and the telephone workers were on strike. The Chicago hard hat unions were dragging their feet in paternal support by delaying the essential wiring of the convention hall, which in turn was affecting the installation and transmission of the brand-new, $40 million state-of-the-art broadcasting equipment just acquired by the networks to cover the convention.

Logistically, the one-square-mile perimeter of the convention area was fenced and capped with barbed wire. Delegates, their spouses, and honored guests found their hotels overbooked, with no alternative lodging inside the designated area. Furthermore, the convention hall itself was grossly under capacity to accommodate either the delegates or the anticipated crowds. There was nowhere to go and no way to get there.

Then there was the issue of coordinating the security forces and which had greater authority. Federally, the Secret Service had one thousand agents on hand to protect the vice president and the presidential candidates who were now issued protective details after Bobby Kennedy's murder. FBI Director J. Edgar Hoover sent one thousand agents to monitor the demonstrators, and 7,500 US Army troops stood ready at nearby bases. Locally, 7,500 men of the Illinois National Guard were made active, and then there were the nearly twelve thousand members of the notorious Chicago "shoot to kill" Police Department, fully supported and defended by Mayor Daley. There was also a three-hundred-man Cook County antiriot squad and two hundred firefighters with high-powered hoses at the ready. It was a recipe for disaster.

Mayor Richard J. Daley was one of the remaining big-city bosses in the United States. Chicago is the biggest city in the Midwest and the third most populated city in the nation. Under Daley, Chicago was a booming industrial hub. The reason Chicago worked so efficiently was because Daley worked so hard to make her that way. He also ruled his metropolis with an iron fist.

First elected mayor in 1955, the son of a steel metal worker, Daley respected both the unions and the white workingman, and they respected him. He effectively suppressed riotous black militant behavior with his shoot-to-kill policy. Daley ran a well-oiled political machine, which pretty much guaranteed a victorious outcome to any candidate it supported, the Daley Democrats.

His political antics were also notorious. When my friend John F. Kennedy Jr. went to Chicago to peddle his political magazine, he quipped about going to the site of his family's two greatest purchases, the Merchandise Mart and his father's 1960 presidential election.

What was unknown by many was that Daley opposed the Vietnam War, but he failed to make it public so as not to bias a nomination in his hometown.

The convention was going to be confusing and complicated. Because of the political drama and social tumult of the Vietnam War and the assassinations of Martin Luther King Jr. and Bobby Kennedy, 1968 had already been a historically horrific year. Now, to make matters worse, just before the convention, the Soviets invaded Czechoslovakia. No matter what the outcome of the convention, there was going to be commotion, but no one could have imagined the unimaginable.

In addition to Democrats, antiwar protestors and political agitators were headed for Chicago in August 1968. Originally the organizers hoped to rally five hundred thousand protestors, prayed for one hundred thousand, but in reality only about thirty thousand showed up. It was a cavalcade of characters; there were pacifists, antiestablishment yippies, Students for a Democratic Society, wandering druggies, McCarthy's college kids, and communist instigators. But there were no black militant groups; they were well aware of Daley's shoot-to-kill orders and avoided the event.

The protestors gathered and encamped to mock the establishment and the government. They humorously nominated a pig for president and just behaved like a bunch of obnoxious frat boys, no big deal. When the cops attempted to control the marching protestors, the demonstrators responded by screaming "*Seig heil!*" Not a wise chant, as I suspect most of these cops were WWII vets. If one goes looking for a confrontation, one usually finds it, but does one really want to aggravate the Chicago Police Department?

The events and drama are legendary, and the topic has been rehashed and retold millions of times. The reality is the kids marched and irritated the cops, the cops overreacted, some punches were thrown, and Chicago became uncivilized. It then got worse.

The next day Daley called up the National Guard. When the protestors raised a North Vietnamese flag, the National Guard took the bait and, with guns drawn, militarily triangulated the protestors into subsets and teargased them. Then the cops mercilessly beat the protestors, to the point that even the pacifists fought back. The press ran clips of bloodied kids getting arrested, shoved into the back of paddy wagons, and screaming the "whole world is watching." And they were right; Daley and his storm troopers were as embarrassing to the Democrats as Lyndon Johnson.

Inside at the convention, another battle was ragging. The Democratic Party needed a platform. The first issue was the war. The second issue was the delegate count. The two largest delegations, New York and California, were both committed to Bobby Kennedy, and he was obviously absent. The third issue was to form a consensus, to craft a platform, and a nominate a candidate.

The first order of business was to support the president, oppose unilateral withdrawal of troops, and stop the bombing of North Vietnam. Accomplished. The second issue was when things turned ugly. There was acrimony on the floor over who controlled Bobby Kennedy's delegates. McCarthy's campaign thought Kennedy's delegates should swing over to McCarthy, and Kennedy's delegates did not give a damn what McCarthy thought. George McGovern was running around trying to mend fences and holding out for Teddy Kennedy to announce his availability. Teddy eventually and quite understandably demurred. It was utter mayhem.

The delegates were getting into fistfights; the security guards patrolling the floor were abusing the press reporting the skirmishes. Daley was raising hell and cutting power to the podium. When Senator Abraham Ribicoff compared the Chicago Police Department's behavior to the Gestapo's, Daley swore at him from the seats, calling him a Jew and a derogatory word that began with the same letter as "faker", which the Daley Camp claimed was the epithet used by the mayor. The chairman was pounding his gavel on the podium for decorum and to adjourn.

The next night was no better. When the tear gas the National Guard used on the protestors got into the air supply system of the buildings, my parents left the convention and returned to their hotel. It was decided that the wives would be spirited off to an important Democratic contributor's Lake Shore Drive penthouse and the men would arrive later when peace was restored.

When the women attempted to exit, the protestors rushed the lobby to evade the club-wielding cops. The elevators were shut down, and the women were trapped inside. My mother, who had managed to successfully exit the fatal Coconut Grove nightclub fire in Boston, was phobic of such events. Somehow they escaped, yet she was not pleased and was not afraid to speak her mind. (After the 1965 inauguration, a male member of this same entourage stood on a table at Paul Young's, the Washington hangout for Kennedy's Irish Mafia, to toast Kennedy's memory and attempted to bring unity to the maudlin group by insulting the newly inaugurated president. My mother, thinking such theatrics duplicitous, grabbed him by his cutaway tails and pulled him down into his seat.)

What happened next is a matter of diverse speculation and fragments of facts, hearsay, and rumor, but no less hysterical. Apparently because of the cramped space at the convention hall, the hotel suites were the epicenters of action and influence. Groups from each camp moved around, searching for ideas, support, delegates, drinks, free food, and access to the powers that be. Again, perfect pandemonium.

During one of these visits, a Daley precinct leader appeared in a suite of Kennedy loyalists from Boston and appealed to the group about the behavior of the "peaceniks." A heated discussion took place regarding the Chicago police tactics. The precinct captain then insulted the group for being too soft and produced a pistol to emphasize his point. Unfortunately for him, this group was as tough as nails and did not appreciate the sight of a handgun in a political environment in deference to Bobby Kennedy. The handgun was forcibly taken away from the Daley delegate, who was shown an inverted view of the Chicago skyline, twenty floors up.

Early the next morning, the men, cautious of their surroundings and standings, exited the hotel and meet the wives at the contributor's penthouse. The women, one can imagine, were mad as hell. Still dressed in elaborate outfits and far away from their cosmetic cases, they were disheveled from sleeping in their dresses on couches and chairs. My mother demanded to return to Boston, and a few others agreed. In order to keep peace and get back to nominating a candidate, the men accommodated the wives. There were more sharp words. In the end, my mother made it home, but she was not in a good mood. When my father returned home after having worked with Mr. O'Donnell to get Humphrey and Maine Senator Edmund Muskie on the ticket, he was a little sheepish around my mother for a week or two. The conversations and rehashing of events at the convention went on for weeks on the front yard of our Cape Cod home.

Finally, late one night I joined my father on that front lawn to look at the stars as he smoked his Lucky Strikes and drank his summer cocktail, and I inquired about what went on in Chicago. He told me that it was a battle like he had never seen before, and it was all over Bobby Kennedy. He said it was a disgrace what happened to him, to the party, and to the country, and we would never be the same. The party was not about us anymore; it was all about what people wanted for themselves. I was confused. He explained, "Imagine if you only wanted what was best for you, not for your country, or the company you work for, but just yourself, and the only way you could get it was to promise someone else all they wanted. It's not about the common good anymore; it's all about politics. People used to have a connection to one another. You knew someone from school or work or church, and you knew she had a brother who needed some help, so you helped him. People were a community then. They looked out for each other, cared about one another, they were connected by some common denominator.

The Democrats tried to nationalize that for everyone, and instead of appreciating it, the greedy wanted more. If you give them an inch, they'll take a mile."

He sounded a lot like Lyndon Johnson: fed up.

13

PICKING UP THE PIECES

Finally the 1968 Democratic National Convention was over. Thank God. Hubert Humphrey and Edmund Muskie had eight weeks to invent a presidential campaign. There was little money, no campaign manager, and the DNC offices were in disarray. There were still Kennedy haters, McCarthy haters, and now Daley Democrat haters. There was much ire and little money. It was still 1968, Johnson was still president, and still flag-draped coffins arrived each day from Vietnam.

JFK's former campaign managers Larry O'Brien and Mr. O'Donnell agreed to assist Humphrey for the sake of the party and because they liked him. In truth, Hubert Humphrey was a good man, yet he remained too loyal to Johnson and for too long. The Humphrey campaign was not organized in the manner that either of the Kennedy men was accustomed to, and with the party so mangled, it was almost hopeless. But they pushed on. Quitting is never an option.

It didn't help that Johnson could not keep his fat mouth shut and let them try to let Humphrey win the election. It is one thing to not be an asset; it is a totally different thing altogether to be a liability. Johnson became a distraction. He kept going on about the Paris peace negotiations, when the campaign was trying to avoid the topic. Things were going to get worse before they got better.

The campaign thought that a Boston rally with Teddy Kennedy welcoming the vice president would be a boost for the campaign coffers and provide some good Democratic footage for a television advertisement. What happened and how the campaign managers, both Massachusetts natives, were so ill prepared for what transpired remains confounding.

Humphrey was not just booed; he was harassed and verbally insulted. Busloads of agitators arrived to shout him down. The Boston police, after the Chicago debacle, were in no mood to be highlighted on the national news and did little to quell the protest. It was a disaster. My father came home mad as hell. He had been there and was appalled by what he saw and heard. In his mind it was official: The country had gone crazy.

The election of 1968 was defined not by Tet or Vietnam, or the assassinations, or the race riots; it was being defined by what happened in Chicago. An ominous Democratic death knell echoed across the nation from Boston, the Cradle of Liberty, the home of the Kennedys, who had sacrificed so much for their party and nation.

Nixon, on the other hand, didn't have to mention what was happening to Humphrey at all. Why get into it? There was no need for defense or attacks. Let the agitators destroy his enemy. Just go on the offense and look like the good guy in comparison. But Nixon was anything but a good guy.

Nixon earned the moniker "Tricky Dick" while campaigning as a Californian congressman transitioning to the Senate. His Democratic opponent, Helen Gahagan Douglas, was a liberal member of Congress. Nixon likened her voting record to that of a suspected communist congressman from New York and printed it on a pink-colored pamphlet. Being a "pinko" was analogous to being a watered-down communist. Nixon liked calling people communists. When Douglas called Nixon a "young man with a dark shirt," a clear reference to Nazis, Nixon replied that he would castrate her. Smart, huh? He later stated "she was pink right down to her underwear." Douglas was defeated by Dick Nixon's dirty tricks, and the label stuck.

Senator Nixon later became Eisenhower's vice president for two terms and later ran for president against JFK in 1960. Returning home to California, he ran for governor, losing to Pat Brown and later claiming the press wasn't going to have "Dick Nixon to kick around anymore."

Now, Nixon had reemerged as the Republican presidential candidate and was preaching "Peace at Home and Peace Abroad." He was also insinuating he had a viable solution to the war but would not reveal it to the American people as the current administration might use it against him. The fact remains that during the closing days of the campaign, Johnson had secured a mutually agreed upon truce at the Paris negotiations, but Nixon used an Asian contact to disrupt the truce, and it fell apart. Johnson called him on it, but it was too late. Eleven senators in the South Vietnam government threw their support to Nixon.

The third-party candidate, antisegregationist Governor George Wallace of University of Alabama infamy, was not taking any votes away from Humphrey, but he was spewing unnecessary hatred and bigotry throughout the land.

Nixon had learned his lesson during the televised debates with Kennedy in 1960, and he refused to debate the garrulous Humphrey. The vice president lambasted Nixon on this point, as well as on his untrustworthiness and unimpressive political record, especially as part of the do-nothing Eisenhower administration, but Nixon would not take him on. Furthermore, the press failed to challenge Nixon on this point and never gave Humphrey the edge on the trust issue. In spite of Humphrey's final breaking with Johnson's foreign policy on Vietnam and a rumored peace accord, which created an increase in polling numbers to within three or four points of Nixon, Humphrey could not, as Harry Truman had done, seal the deal in the final weeks of the election. He lost.

Nixon won with a little more populace edge than he garnered in 1960 but with 50 percent more electoral votes than

Humphrey. Wallace won the Deep South. The Democratic Party of Wilson, Roosevelt, Truman, Kennedy, and now Johnson was history; it was no longer the popular party of America.

Everything changed that year. The only good thing that happened was that in late December, as NASA prepared to fulfill Kennedy's objective of sending a man to the moon and back, spaceflight Apollo 8 left the earth's orbit and entered into the moon's gravitational pull. On Christmas Eve the crew, while looking back at earth, a small blue marble spinning in a universe of darkness, read the first few lines of the Book of Genesis from the Bible. It was the most watched event of its time, yet who would have known, from a quarter of a million miles away, how much hatred, violence, war, and tumult existed on our small planet that year? Good riddance.

14

NIXON & THE KNUCKLEHEADS

So now we have Tricky Dick Nixon in the White House. His "secret plan" to end the war became a fallacy. As suspected, it was an election gimmick. In reality he ran an election to unite America and to stimulate the "silent majority" of conservatives who opposed the war, the liberal agenda of the past two administrations, and the overall direction of the nation. He won on a platform of law and order.

Nixon not only did not end the war, he escalated it. He bombed outside Vietnam and invaded Laos and Cambodia without informing Congress. He sent National Security Adviser Henry Kissinger to the Paris negotiation table with a "madman" scenario insinuating Nixon could go off the wall at any given time and might go so far as to use nuclear weapons to end the war. It was believable, as there was plenty of evidence to support the theory of Nixon as a madman.

Nixon and Kissinger instead came up with a plan to buy them time to surrender with honor, and that was "Vietnamization."

Similar to President Kennedy's policy of having the South Vietnamese fight their own damn war, Nixon wanted to halt US ground troop casualties by having the Vietnamese fight the war on the battlefield while the US bombed the hell out of the North from the air. And did he bomb. There was more tonnage of bombs dropped on North Vietnam by US forces than during both world wars combined.

The college kids continued to protest for the end of the war. At Kent State in May 1970, the Ohio Army National Guard fired live ammunition at college students protesting the illegal invasion of Cambodia, killing four and wounding nine. The nation was frozen with the disastrous realities of Nixon.

The inevitable reality in my house was that my father was soon going to be out of a job, so he dug in his heels. When the new director of the SBA visited him at his Boston office, he was surprised to find that not only was my father not accepting of the news, but he planned to put up a fight. Before the new boss left, he instructed my father to take down the official presidential portraits of Kennedy and Johnson and put up one of the new president. He did; it was an eight-by-ten-inch portrait of Nixon. He called it the "laughing hyena" and placed it next to a bookcase so that even a professional scavenger hunter would have a difficult time locating it. Oh, and the enormous Kennedy and Johnson portraits continued to hang side by side at the end of the conference table.

Later, dear old Dad received notice that he was going to be demoted and relocated to Washington, DC. My father did not like Washington; he commuted there during the week for the past eight years but always came home at his earliest convenience. In response, he made a vague reference to SBA funds flowing out of the Miami office to Nixon's best friend Bebe Robazzo's enterprises, and the heat came off for a while. Then it would boil up again, and he found a union official or a representative from the Federal Executive Board who filed a complaint that a director could not be demoted and relocated simultaneously, and they would back off again.

Finally he was ordered to Washington in the summer of 1970, and he was not happy about it. With the new administration, all his old friends were now gone. He had a "lousy little apartment" and listened to sirens wail all night long. New anti-crime streetlights had been installed all over Washington, and the orange glow kept him awake at night. Furthermore, for anyone who has not spent a summer in the swamp that now houses our nation's capital, it's a steam bath.

After Labor Day, he put it on the line. "Either fire me, or I'm going home to Boston," and then he got on a plane. Kenny O'Donnell was running for governor, and if he could get him elected, all would be well. Needless to say, neither ended as hoped. My father opened an office and reentered the medical supply industry.

The green phone in his den still rang, and I still eavesdropped. One Sunday night Senator Muskie called my father. He and Muskie had become close, not just because of the federal position, but the Boston-to-Washington shuttle originated in Bangor, Maine, and they sat together during the flight. When Muskie asked for his support in an election attempt to unseat Nixon, my father apologized and stated that he had already committed to Birch Bayh, but if anything changed, he would keep him in mind. As always when that phone rang, a homespun political discussion would follow. He was explaining the conversation to my mother. Stumped for an answer to one of her questions, he called to me. Thinking I was in trouble for listening in, I came down the stairs red-faced. "Billy, what did he say about Wisconsin?" He knew I was listening all along. Now with immunity, I asked who was Birch Bayh. "The next president of the United States, if I can do anything about it," my father replied.

My father never saw that election of 1972. He died before the primaries began, three months after being diagnosed with cancer. When he was sick at home, his buddies would come and visit. Kenny was writing a book about his experience with JFK, *Johnny, We Hardly Knew Ye,* and they would reminisce about the good old days. I listened in, a sponge for their knowledge and experience. I knew he was going to die, and I wanted to remember everything they said and joked about.

It was still a shock when he died. I was only thirteen. Paul Kirk called from the West Coast. He was traveling with Teddy

Kennedy and called to express their sympathy. My mother had me on the other line; Teddy talked about Brookline and "all he had done for my brothers." I was choked with emotion. At the wake, all the good old guys came: Dave Powers, the former and future speakers of the house, the Massachusetts delegation, cops, firemen, Irish cousins my father sponsored into the country. His Irish mother keened, and I cried. The next day after the funeral, Kenny O'Donnell and Jim Carr picked me up to attend the Princeton-Harvard game. They told me that it was the game they always went to with my father. They also told me that now that my father was gone, I had to move on with my life, that is what he would have wanted. And I did.

Nixon continued with his political games, fueled by paranoia. He was reelected by a landslide in 1972. Massachusetts and Washington, DC, were the only two electoral district votes he did not receive. Aside from the evidence from CREEP of his predictable landslide, Nixon was still mentally unstable enough to have his "plumbers" break into the DNC offices at the executive complex known as the Watergate. Ha. The freak could not help himself.

Nixon's second term was a disaster. He never clarified his position on Vietnam. He bombed the hell out of North Vietnam at Christmas 1972. Two *Washington Post* reporters scratched the surface of the Watergate break-in and found a treasure trove of cover-up material and illegalities originating in the Oval Office.

Vice President Spiro Agnew resigned from office for accepting illegal bribes while governor of Maryland. Under the rules of the recently updated Twenty-fifth Amendment, Nixon needed a new vice president. He selected Gerald R. Ford of Michigan, a highly respected Eagle Scout, All-American football player, and the current minority leader in the House of Representatives, to fill the slot.

When the unrelenting Watergate inquiries finally got to him, Nixon had a hissy fit. Obviously under the influence of drugs or alcohol, or both, a slurring Nixon addressed the nation, stating, "I am not a crook." He was of course lying. He was a crook, and so were his cronies. Attorney General John Mitchell, who ran both his recent presidential campaigns and held the highest legal office in the land, was sentenced to jail, as were other members of his White House staff.

What did work in Nixon's favor was the probable "corrupt bargain" he struck with Gerald Ford. Once Ford became the nation's first nonelected president, he used his presidential powers of executive clemency to pardon Nixon. Three years later, Ford was the baby thrown out with Nixon's bathwater. Ha.

15

A FORD, NOT
A LINCOLN

According to the Constitution, the president of the United States is head of the executive branch of government, which is equipped with the standard checks and balances that efficiently operate our democracy. For example, the president appoints federal judges, and Congress confirms or denies his appointments. The president in turn may veto congressional bills, yet Congress may override his veto with a two-thirds majority. The president may also issue broad-based executive orders and is commander in chief of the armed forces. He also possesses executive clemency, the power to pardon.

Ford's use of executive clemency for the "full, free, and absolute" pardon of Richard Nixon in September 1974 caused a firestorm of negative reaction across the nation. There were rumors of collusion at the highest level. The *New York Times* wrote, "If clemency had followed conviction rather than preceded it, there would have been wide acceptance of President Ford's exercise of his power to pardon." With clemency, an arrogant and unapologetic Nixon never explained himself to the nation.

Politically this was catastrophic for Republicans. In the midterm elections three months later, the Democrats won the majority in both the House and Senate, and maintained the coveted two-thirds majority in the House that could override presidential vetoes. Furthermore, this mandate restrained the future use of the armed forces by the commander in chief.

The War Powers Act, initiated and passed by Congress, now regulated that the president, as commander in chief, could deploy use of armed forces only for thirty days without further explanation or approval from Congress.

Ford, like his five predecessors, still faced the consequences of Vietnam. Although the North Vietnamese had signed a peace agreement with the United States, they failed to adhere to its provisions and slowly seeped into South Vietnam. Ford appealed to Congress for military aid and was promptly denied. In March 1975 Saigon was overthrown and renamed Ho Chi Minh City. Later that month, Ford ended the draft. The Vietnam War was finally over. It took an unelected president to allow it all to end.

The twenty-year struggle in Vietnam resulted in huge financial debts and unnecessary human currency. In the years between 1965 and 1975, 111 billion of taxpayers' dollars were spent on the war, and 58,220 US troops were killed in action, 150,000 were wounded, and 21,000 were permanently disabled. A million Vietnamese were dead. Our hopes to contain, if not end, the spread of communism in Vietnam had failed. Laos and Cambodia soon followed. The domino effect theorists of the 1950s were correct: Southeast Asia was now "Red."

At home, Ford faced many economic challenges. Nixon had taken the nation off the gold standard in August 1971, and the cost of commodities increased. Real estate values increased, and automobiles became more costly, meaning the consumer was less likely to replace his car every two years, as had been the norm. OPEC was controlling the spigot of available oil supplies and the price of gasoline was rising steeply. Energy issues were plaguing the nation, and inflation was skyrocketing. In fact it was the greatest recession since the Great Depression. The Equal Rights Amendment made it easier for housewives to enter the labor force, and many US families became dual income to keep up with inflation.

In 1976, the United States celebrated its bicentennial. Gerald Ford presided over the nation's two-hundredth birthday on July Fourth and hosted multiple international dignitaries and events. Later that celebratory summer, he left the Republican National Convention with not only the nomination, but also a roughly thirty-point lead over the virtually unknown Democratic candidate, former governor of Georgia Jimmy Carter.

For the first time since 1960, televised presidential debates took place. Up until the second debate, Jimmy Carter, having made questionable personal errors during the primary season, remained a weak opponent. During the second debate, President Ford announced, "There is no Soviet domination of Eastern Europe, and there never will be under a Ford administration." A befuddled nation scratched its head and wondered if Ford had been asleep for the past twenty-five years.

Saturday Night Live's Chevy Chase mocked Ford mercilessly about being a buffoon in over his head, being clumsy, and generally playing too much football without a helmet. Ford gave Chase plenty of ammunition to lampoon him every week, when the whole nation was watching. Carter won the election with over 50 percent of the popular vote, the first president elected from the Deep South since Zachary Taylor in 1848.

Ford was so emotional over the loss he could not make a concession speech, and advisers were concerned he might become suicidal. Later Ford became so enraged at his defeat that he turned on the government and, in disregarding Harry Truman's protocol of protecting the people's office of the president, declared, "Now it is my turn," and joined several corporate boards and played golf under the watch of a full detail of Secret Service agents. He said it himself: "I'm a Ford, not a Lincoln."

16

MIXED NUTS

James Earl Carter Jr. is a good and a humble man. He graduated from the United States Naval Academy and served as an officer in WWII. After the war, he returned home to Plains, Georgia, to rescue his father's struggling peanut farm. Carter entered politics in the heady 1960s and served in the Georgia State Senate and later was elected governor. Jimmy Carter was successful in many pursuits, but not as president.

In 1976, Jimmy Carter was an unusual alternative to Gerald Ford, but the nation was seeking to purge itself from anything related to Nixon or Watergate. American voters were so hungry for new leadership that they steered clear of career politicians in Washington and elected a "born again" Baptist from the Deep South as their new president.

During the primary season, candidate Carter took on a crowded field of over a dozen well-known Washington Democrats and quickly found the lead. His grassroots campaign staff, the "Peanut Brigade," traveled the country, sleeping in cars, cheap motel rooms, and guest bedrooms, to hype

Carter's promises to be good, to be honest, and not to lie. He was the voice of honesty in the wake of Nixon's felonies.

Much to everyone's amazement, Carter won the Iowa caucus. What made this extraordinary was no one had ever heard of the Iowa caucus. Yet with a "win" in their pockets, the Peanut Brigade moved to frosty New Hampshire for the first primary.

I was a prep school student in New Hampshire that season and had some friends at nearby Dartmouth College. Since the voting age had been lowered to eighteen a few years before, the field of candidates was cultivating millions of now-eligible college voters. We took in rallies, did a bit of Q&A, and discussed the strengths and weaknesses of each candidate. Carter was the clear favorite of college students.

Carter's stunning victory in the New Hampshire primary made the previously unknown candidate the party's frontrunner. Much to the delight of the press, a Southerner winning a Northern primary made for good copy, and the caricature of grinning peanut farmer made for invaluable editorial cartoon material.

Carter did not win all the primaries, but his campaign train just kept on chugging along. By the time I graduated and headed home, Carter had pretty much sealed the nomination. Having just celebrated my eighteenth birthday, I went down to my local town hall—in the same town I live in now—and proudly registered myself as a voter and a Democrat. It felt as if I had enlisted in the service of my country. I was so proud of my party affiliation and could not wait to cast my vote; finally I belonged to the Democratic Party.

I cast my vote for Carter that November and he won. I was delighted with myself. I had friends who worked for Carter that summer who were subsequently invited to the inauguration. When they showed me the invitation, I was surprised to find it was not the elegantly scripted and boldly embossed formal invitation I had seen from previous inaugurations, but a tacky tan script on beige recycled paper. It referred to the president-elect as "Jimmy Carter" instead of his full and proper name. *Beige* was a harbinger of things to come.

President Carter's pettiness soon became a character flaw. He refused to allow the Secret Service to handle his luggage, a security risk, and prohibited bands from playing "Hail to the Chief" upon his arrival. I knew right away we had been suckered. Carter was a poor boy in a rich man's house. Carter cut his own budget, and Washington insiders became increasingly annoyed with his frugality.

When Carter held breakfast meetings at the White House, he served muffins instead of the traditional bacon and eggs. He stopped serving alcohol in the White House. He sold the fleet of luxurious presidential yachts, allowing speculators to buy them and turn impressive profits commercializing them as historical attractions. He gave up control of the Panama Canal and returned Saint Stephen's crown to the Hungarians during communist occupation. He was micromanaging trivial issues, and the Washington elite was not impressed.

I was in Dublin, Ireland studying Western European politics in the spring of 1977. Each day the American students fought over the *International Herald Tribune* to find out what was going on at home. It was not inspiring. Some thought that the international press was being harsh on Carter because he was so down-to-earth and foreign correspondents could be snobby and dismissive of American upstarts. But the handwriting was on the wall; Carter was clearly in over his head. As he battled the energy crisis, he turned down the thermostat in the White House, put on a cardigan, held fireside chats, and installed solar panels on the roof on the White House. It was so simplistic it was painful to watch.

About a month into office, Press Secretary Jody Powell called upon an acquaintance of mine on Capitol Hill to visit him at the White House. Powell explained how overwhelmed the Carter staff was in Washington and asked if he would consider coming to work at the White House as a congressional liaison. This political associate of mine pointed out to Powell how the Hill was diminutively viewing the new administration for its lack of communication with Congress. Furthermore, to leave his professional position on the Hill and transfer to an incompetent White House was not only an act of sacrilege, it was political suicide. Powell admitted that the administration was lax in communication with Congress and proceeded to open a cabinet with over thirty thousand pieces of unanswered congressional mail, which is taboo in Washington. He declined Powell's offer in astonishment.

The Nixon administration had reinforced the historical premise that an imperial presidency was too powerful and asymmetrical for a well-balanced democracy. By being inept, the Carter White House was unwittingly resuscitating the enormous institutional power of the House of Representatives. The new speaker, Massachusetts native son Tip O'Neill, seemed to flourish during the Carter administration. In post-Watergate Washington, there were many newly elected Democrats. Some of the recent arrivals were subversive or naive and thus lacked party loyalty. O'Neill helped them find their way. With both House and Senate and the White House all Democratic, this was an epic opportunity to accomplish much, but Carter remained fixated on the minutiae.

There were big-ticket issues on hand. Strategic Arms Limitation Talks (SALT) negotiations were under way with the Soviets. There was an energy crisis as the result of the OPEC cartel and continued diplomatic weakness in the Middle East. Apparently a party elder, for the betterment of the nation, got to Carter and guided him through his quagmire. The SALT treaties were signed, a Cabinet post was established to deal with energy issues, and Carter took the leaders of Israel and Egypt to Camp David and hammered out the Middle East peace accords. Things were happening, and things appeared good.

Carter deregulated the airlines and bailed out Chrysler. He increased the number of naval vessels in both oceans, inspired "no nukes" concerts that promoted alternative energy, and promoted international human rights. A New Age subculture materialized, and the nation seemed enlightened by the holistic evolution.

But the Democratic leadership remained underwhelmed. Whoever got to Carter and gave him direction was now telling tales out of school. It was determined by Washington insiders that Carter was weak, a waffler who was too quick to back down from negotiations and who ignored the tenor of the robust and cornucopian Congress.

Soon the wheels began to come off the Carter administration; inflation hit 14 percent, the prime rate increased to 20 percent, there was high unemployment, and gas prices doubled. Then things started to go bad, really bad. By 1978 Teddy Kennedy was making foreign policy deals with the Soviets under the premise of removing Carter from office. Additionally, Kennedy pulled his support of Carter's national health care initiative, always Kennedy's *raison d'être*, as a strategy to make Carter appear weak. Publicly, Carter complied; he collapsed during a 5K run and claimed he was attacked by a vicious river rabbit while fishing. The press was having a field day. He quickly became the caricature of the primaries, a goofy and toothy southern hick, think of Gomer Pyle.

Along with the unflattering press clippings, the global forum sensed his incapacitated authority. Revolutionaries around the world, under the auspices of being freedom fighters for Carter's human rights platform, began acting up. The Irish Republican Army, the Palestine Liberation Organization, Black September, the Japanese Red Army, Cubans in Angola, the Red Brigade in Italy, the Shining Path in Peru, the Khmer Rouge in Cambodia, and the Babbar Khalsa International in India were all escalating bombing campaigns with endemic versions of organized terror.

There were political assassinations, kidnappings, bombings, and hijackings. It was as if Carter had unleashed a fever of international mayhem not witnessed in recent years. The Cold War was becoming frigid again, and the world was becoming more unstable. The Soviets invaded Afghanistan, and our ambassador there was kidnapped and killed. Carter's deft response was to boycott the 1980 Summer Olympics in Moscow.

Then there was the crescendo of international struggles in the Middle East. Radical Islamic students overthrew our ally, the Shah of Iran. Antimonarchist acrimony had been festering for years in Iran. Its people thought the monarchy was excessively influenced by non-Muslim America and, as such, was diluting their Islamic culture. I was in Washington in the summer of 1977 when the Shah visited Carter in the White House. Iranian students chanted the "Shah is a US puppet" and rushed the White House fences. It was a hot, sticky, eye-stinging day as the waves of riot-issued teargas drifted across the White House lawn.

While Iranians suffered from extreme shortages and high inflation, the royal family lived an opulent and lavish lifestyle within the confines of the royal palace. There was evidence of widespread political corruption and accusations of brutality by the Shah's secret police for those who complained. An exiled Islamic cleric, Ayatollah Khomeini, called for an Islamic revolution, and the Shah's monarchy was overthrown by religious extremists in early 1979.

That autumn, at the request of prominent Americans, the cancer-ridden Shah was allowed to enter the United States for treatment at the Mayo Clinic. In Tehran, the student protesters went berserk and attacked the US Embassy. Carter ordered the Marine Corps Embassy Security Group to stand down and not defend the embassy, which is sovereign US soil. This was not an easy concept for Marines, but they complied with the orders from their commander in chief.

With impunity, the students climbed the walls of the embassy, overran the building, and took the staff hostage. The insurgents paraded the blindfolded Marines in front of the international press, denigrated the American flag, and burned Carter in effigy. A wave of patriotism swept across the United States. Carter continually failed to negotiate a release of the hostages with Khomeini, who now returned to Iran and denounced America as the "Great Satan."

Teddy Kennedy & Jimmy Carter

Courtesy: Jimmy Carter Presidential Library

Teddy Kennedy had had enough of Carter's incompetence and quickly announced his candidacy for president. Maybe too quickly. When asked by CBS correspondent Roger Mudd "Why do you want to be president?" Kennedy could not concoct a coherent answer. The usually verbose Kennedy, a seasoned politician who had endured so many public tragedies, who usually came up with an intelligent and thoughtful response, fumbled the ball. During the interview, the program ran a dramatization of Kennedy's infamous Chappaquiddick car accident, which reminded the nation of Kennedy's alleged infidelities and rumored personal irresponsibility that took a young girl's life. It was going to be tough sledding.

It also did not help that Carter would not leave the White House to campaign or even debate Kennedy. Carter stayed in the Rose Garden, making press statements and hiding behind his rosebushes like a timid weakling, petrified of the big bully, Teddy Kennedy, patrolling Pennsylvania Avenue calling for Carter to come out and fight like a man. As the primary season wore on and Carter continued to fail to negotiate with the Iranians, the Kennedy campaign gained momentum.

Carter's "malaise speech" a few months before, what he called a "Crisis of Confidence," had caused the nation to pause. Americans do not like to be scolded or belittled; they prefer to be led. This televised speech validated Carter as a judgmental, condescending, and self-righteous mollycoddle lacking presidential hubris.

Out of frustration or humiliation, Carter attempted a rescue mission for the hostages held in Tehran. When he presented the plan to the Joint Chiefs of Staff, each lobbied for his military branch to lead the exercise. Carter, in true form, vacillated and agreed that Operation Eagle Claw should be a combined rescue mission. Having never practiced such an maneuver, a breach of communication caused the team of helicopters to collide in the Iranian dessert. Eight US troops were killed and many badly burned. Commander in Chief Carter failed to give a direct and efficient military order.

Carter was globally embarrassed and portrayed as an indecisive and over analyzing weakling. The USA was loosing international respect and credibility. Carter's approval polls plummeted to below Nixon's resignation nadir. As a result, Kennedy began to win primaries, but it was too little to late; he had not gathered enough delegates to secure the nomination.

It was a nasty and bitter convention. Kennedy tried to get Carter's delegates released and open the convention, but he failed. It was the first campaign loss by a Kennedy. Teddy's concession speech remains the most impressive speech about the Democratic Party I ever heard anyone deliver.

"The serious issue before us tonight is the cause for which the Democratic Party has stood in its finest hours, the cause that keeps our party young and makes it, in the second century of its age, the largest political party in this republic and the longest-lasting political party on this planet. Our cause has been, since the days of Thomas Jefferson, the cause of the common man and the common woman...As Democrats we recognize that each generation of Americans has a rendezvous with a different reality...The answers of one generation become the questions of the next generation. For all those whose cares have been our concern, the work goes on, the cause endures, the hope still lives, and the dream shall never die."

With all his good and moral intentions, like his brother Bobby, Teddy Kennedy opposed a sitting Democratic president and split the party, allowing Republican Ronald Reagan to verify how rudderless the Democrats really were. Carter became the first one-term Democrat since before the Civil War.

Something had happened to America in the 1970s, and it was not just politics and presidents—it was more than that. There was a platonic shift in society. The previous generation of leaders was retired, dead, or disgraced. Unusual policies of affirmative action, abortion, and forced busing were prevailed upon the public, and there was rampant knee-jerk social dissatisfaction.

Somehow an executive order from the Kennedy-Johnson era known as affirmative action surfaced as a social dynamic in the mid-1970s. Initially scripted to promote equal opportunity for minorities and to eliminate discriminatory practices on federally funded projects, its practical application created a spontaneous retort that smacked of reverse discrimination. Simply put, minorities were granted unequal access to employment opportunities due to implied institutional and societal exploitation in the past, and to add insult to injury, it was invoked at the expense of the nonminority (white) labor force. As with Social Security, federal civil rights directives had to be available to all, not just a few, otherwise the absence of civil rights is discrimination.

Eventually this practice spilled over into local municipal hiring. Minorities who scored lower on standardized tests were given preferential treatment by the hiring institution as a result of the federal precept. Occupations that require technical training for critically dependent situations, such as firefighters or police officers, were awarded to less capable recipients due to a perceived historical persecution based on the color of their skin. This was not equal access—it was institutionalized racism.

Without dexterous critics, affirmative action seeped into public colleges and universities. Federal grants were promised and awarded to private universities and graduate schools that embraced the policy. Again, lower-scoring applicants were awarded preferential treatment in advanced critical industries such as medicine and law based on graduate school openings reserved for minorities.

Reverse-discrimination lawsuits popped up all over the country, from firehouses, to playgrounds, to medical schools. Cultural resentment and racial division became intensified as affirmative action expanded into the economics of all social stratums. To the white man, the loss of a job offer or a promotion to a less qualified black man was referred to with a repugnant racial slur, the antithesis of the original executive order.

I remember one afternoon when I was a kid on Cape Cod when an acquaintance of a family member approached my father in a public restaurant for an SBA loan to fund a building project. Although it was not the proper location for such a discussion, my father listened. Afterward my father explained to the inquirer if his project met the guidelines for a low-interest government-backed loan, it was required that a certain percentage of minorities were hired for the project. The builder asked my father if he knew any black electricians or plumbers whom he could hire to meet the criteria. My father politely explained that based on his condescending comments, it would probably be best if he sought an alternate strategy. The builder stated that he already attempted that and was denied. My father was not surprised.

Years earlier Teddy Kennedy sent a local minority business-man to see my father about an SBA loan. Although his business was sound, it did not meet the guidelines for a government loan. In the spirit of the times and out of respect to the sena-tor's request, my father decided to fund the operation on his own. The loan was repaid ahead of schedule. True business-men know the value of a man's worth and the service he pro-vides; they are not influenced by the color of his skin.

Abortion also became a lightning rod in 1970s culture. A woman's privacy was guaranteed by the Supreme Court in Roe v. Wade, under the due process clause of the Fourteenth Amendment, and afforded her the choice to have an abortion. Forty years later the merits of this case remains curiously topi-cal and controversial by social and religious organizations. The bottom line is that abortion is the law and it is a woman's per-sonal prerogative. Pro-choice groups claim that if men could get pregnant, abortion would not be just a law but a sacrament. I disagree but appreciate the concept of individual choice and adherence to the law. I also believe that if one does not want an abortion, one should not get pregnant. Birth control is readily available to those informed enough to use it, but please do not use abortion as a form of birth control and don't tell me that partial-birth abortions are not infanticide. Furthermore, as with any medical procedure, abortions for underage girls should require parental permission. Let us be reasonable on such a highly charged issue.

Also in the 1970s, Washington liberals continued to push social activism. Teddy Kennedy was one of the biggest proponents for forced busing. When the practice came to Boston, the hometown of the Kennedy clan, white Irish Catholic South Boston became unhinged and threw gasoline on the flames of racial bigotry. As an Irish Catholic Democrat, I could not believe what the South Boston citizens, the ones with the pictures of JFK and the pope hanging on their walls, had to say about Teddy Kennedy, his family, and the black community. It was racism at its worst, and another good intention gone terribly wrong.

It was a hot topic. I was a guest at Kennedy's Washington home over a long weekend while busing was being forced in Boston. He talked with me about the law and what it aimed to accomplish. He was right. If whites and blacks were ever going to coexist, it was best to begin the process during the formative years. I got it, no problem. But not in South Boston, anywhere but "Southie." It just did not work, and the battle went on for years. There are many sociological studies published that support both points of view, but it boils down to this: Don't bus my kids to an inferior elementary school in the black section of Boston, and don't bus black kids into my multigenerational neighborhood schools. Two generations later, Southie is slightly more diverse and accepting, but not nearly as integrated as Kennedy had hoped, and as a result, the public schools are now subpar.

Maybe it was the hangover from the sixties, the sobering of the hallucinating drug culture, but as marriages failed and divorces skyrocketed, the family unit dissolved. Entertainment became pornographic and gratuitously violent. Music changed; instead of Motown, we listened to disco. Cars changed; instead of Detroit-manufactured convertibles and muscle cars with enormous horsepower, we were offered generic, fuel-efficient, foreign-made tin cans. America had lost its exceptionalism. We no longer drove Chevy ragtops, while listening to rock 'n' roll, to the drive-in; we drove Tin Lizzies from Japan and listened to British techno-pop on the way to the McDonald's drive-thru window.

As crime rates rose, America looked back in time, to a quieter and more orderly period, before Nixon, Watergate, Vietnam, and assassinations. Before race riots and provocative lifestyles. The popular 1970s television show *Happy Days* had America yearning for those days of grandfatherly Eisenhower and simple Midwest pleasures. It was time to put even Carter behind us; he was, in actuality, the consolation to the nation's electoral reaction to Watergate.

In response, the United States elected a former film star and former governor, Ronald Reagan, as our new chief executive. Reagan didn't win by just a landslide. It was a bloody massacre. Reagan was declared the winner before the polls had closed in his home state of California. Carter received about

10 percent of the Electoral College votes. It was the greatest popular defeat ever. The Republicans not only unseated an incumbent president but also secured a majority in the Senate, the first time in twenty-five years.

I could not vote for Carter; I loathed what he had done to the party. He cultivated an atmosphere of condescending high morality, promoted victimization, and failed to defend us against terror. I voted for Congressman John Anderson of Illinois. It is amazing how things can change in four short years.

17

RAWHIDE & REAL MEN RIDE AGAIN

What can I say? Carter was inept, and Ronald Reagan was a broken-down old movie star at best. In my mind, we were screwed. When Reagan was sixty-nine years old when he was elected in president in 1980. He was older than JFK, if he were alive, who was president a score of years previous. The adage is when the nation votes for Republicans, they elect a trusted grandfatherly type. When they vote for Democrats, they elect a cool, hip uncle. To me, Reagan was nearly prehistoric.

The 1980 election was unique to all other elections. Reagan was not only aged, but he was a former Democrat turned Republican. "I didn't leave the Democratic Party. The party left me," he said. Yet he won the election by converting loyal Democrats to vote for him. "Reagan Democrats" were fed up with losing wars and national prestige, fiscal irresponsibility, affirmative action, government regulations, and the likes of Jimmy Carter. Reagan was an old-school, hard-line conservative. He preached family values, yet he was our first divorced president with two sets of children, and the second set barely even spoke with him.

We also voted out a sitting president, not just because he was inept and in way over his head, not because he took the nation for a circus ride, or because his own party leaders spilt the ticket. The real reason we kicked Carter out of office was the fifty-two American hostages held in the basement of our embassy in Tehran.

The moment that Reagan took the oath of office, declaring in his inaugural address, "Government is not the solution to our problems. It is the problem," the Ayatollah was releasing the hostages after 444 days in captivity. Why? Because the Iranians were scared to death of Ronald Reagan, and there was good reason to be.

Ronald Reagan was a man of his word. If he said it, he meant it, and if it were a threat, he would follow through on it. He ran for governor of California in 1966 stating he wanted to get "bums" off welfare and clean up the "mess" at USC-Berkeley, a Mecca for far-left liberal protestors. In May 1969, he declared a state of emergency at Berkeley and sent in 2,700 National Guardsman, along with local law enforcement groups, in full riot gear. They beat the crap out of the protestors, fired tear gas, and even used shotguns on the crowds. In what became known as "Bloody Thursday," one man was killed and another blinded by the buckshot. Reagan stated, "If it takes a bloodbath, let's get it over with. No more appeasement." Pacifist Joan Baez referred to him as "Ronald Rayguns."

Although Reagan was a death penalty advocate, as governor he signed an abortion bill into law. He also signed the first no-fault divorce legislation in the nation. He disapproved of laws restricting homosexuals from working in public schools. He may have been a conservative, but he was a California conservative. He attempted to grasp the Republican nomination away from Gerald Ford in 1976, to no avail, but by 1980, he was tanned, rested, and ready.

Just as Jimmy Carter defeated Teddy Kennedy by hiding in the Rose Garden, he now refused to debate Reagan during the election process. Finally Carter succumbed and attempted to profile Reagan as a warmongering hawk. But when Carter quoted his twelve-year-old daughter's thoughts on nuclear arms, Reagan dismissively laughed at him and asked the people of America if they were better off than they were four years ago. Even Eugene McCarthy, the dove from 1968, endorsed Reagan, stating Carter was the "worst" president in history. Reagan won the election with over 50 percent of the popular vote.

The "Reagan Revolution" began immediately after he took the oath of office. He sought lower taxes to stimulate the economy; he believed in less government, more states rights, a strong national defense, and returning the US to the gold standard. He was a powerhouse who hired a powerful team of administrators, Cabinet members, and advisers. Even JFK's widow commented that Reagan's presidency was going to be the first effective administration since her husband's thousand days in office.

Soon into his first term, Reagan was wounded in an assassination attempt. Called the "Curse of Tecumseh," starting with William Henry Harrison, who was elected in 1840, every president elected in a "0" year had died in office. Reagan survived the attack and ended the curse. He laughed it off, saying to his frantic wife, "I forgot to duck."

He ended many things in his budget cuts. Reagan's FY1982 budget proposed $57 billion in spending cuts, with $27 billion of those to entitlements. He looked to reduce federally funded lunches that required a vegetable by $1 billion, and he designated ketchup as a vegetable. I wore a button that was very trendy in the early eighties that stated, "Ketchup is not a vegetable." Democrats and Republicans began living in two entirely different Americas.

At first it appeared that the administration's supply-side economic policies, which became known as "Reaganomics," were not going to work out as planned. Inflation and unemployment remained high during his first two years as president. Undeterred by sagging polls, the administration sought to reduce government programs and introduced the largest across-the-board tax cuts in history.

Then things began to change, almost overnight. Unemployment dropped, interest rates dropped, the Dow Jones Industrial Average index closed above one thousand for the first time ever, and citizens were making money. When Reagan went too far, Tip O'Neill would step in and put him back in place. Reagan came up with some crazy ideas, but they seemed to work. He was known as the Teflon president; nothing bad stuck to him.

When Reagan proposed the Strategic Defense Initiative (SDI), which would essentially create a shield over America from outer space to protect us from nuclear missile attack, Teddy Kennedy coined the initiative "Star Wars." Reagan was mocked for SDI as if it were some dime-novel science fiction fabrication, but it scared the hell out of the Soviet Union, which did not know what to make of Reagan, his military build-ups, or Star Wars.

Globally, Reagan began rattling his presidential saber. He was defiant toward the Soviets and dropped the policy of detente. He ordered the US armed forces beefed up and accelerated development of military weapons that were abandoned by Carter. When the Soviets deployed new missiles, he sent more of ours into NATO Germany. He disgustedly walked out of negotiations with Soviet leaders when he felt he was not making headway. He referred to the USSR as the "Evil Empire" and predicted that communism would collapse, stating, "Communism is another sad, bizarre chapter in human history whose last pages even now are being written." He sent the CIA into Afghanistan to fight the Soviets and into areas of Latin America, Asia, and Africa. He was fearless, and he was not going to get pushed around. "Of the four wars in my lifetime, none came about because the US was too strong," he said.

An even greater landslide than four years before reelected him. He won every state in the nation except for his opponent's home state. In his second term, he continued to beat the war drums. He attacked Libya after a US-targeted bombing, and he challenged the Soviet premier to "tear down this wall" as he stood next to the Berlin Wall.

Reagan was out of office when the wall did come down, but in reflection, the Soviet premier humbly admitted it was because of Reagan and Star Wars that the wall did come down and that the Soviet Union did collapse, ending the Leninist-Marxist grasp of Eastern Europe. Ronald Reagan is a modern-day hero.

When Ronald Reagan was first voted into office, I was a caseworker at the Massachusetts Department of Public Welfare. I saw firsthand the abuses of the welfare programs that my Democratic heroes had put into place. By graduation, my college classmates were being hired by Wall Street broker-age houses. As I was tired of taking public transportation and watching welfare families perpetuate their dependence of entitlement programs, I joined the private sector. Within no time I was paying more in income taxes as a stockbroker than I earned as a welfare worker.

I was still a registered Democrat, but now a fiscally conservative one. I was schooled to "think Democrat, vote Republican."
I never called myself a Reagan Democrat, but I stopped calling
myself a Kennedy Democrat, as the connotation now was for
Teddy's brand of politics rather than the JFK standard, and
they had little in common. It dawned on me that in the absence
of being a liberal Democrat; one does not have to morph into a
conservative Republican.

18

DUDLEY DO-RIGHT & THE DUKE

Conservative pundit George Will once stated that Vice President George H.W. Bush was Ronald Reagan's lapdog. He was. George Bush is the consummate preppy, educated at Andover and Yale, the son of a US senator. For years, George Bush orbited the world of politics and presidential administrations. Virtually unknown to the general public, he ran against Reagan in the 1980 primaries. He denounced Reagan's supply-side theories as "voodoo" economics. When Reagan called him out for a face-to-face debate in New Hampshire, Bush failed to show up. Reagan thought him a political coward but in the end sought his loyalty and offered to share the Republican ticket with him.

After two terms as Reagan's vice president, Bush announced his own intentions to run for president. *Newsweek* branded him a "wimp." Somehow the moniker's definition evolved from a timid, mild-mannered, milquetoast type of fellow to the WASP persona of George H.W. Bush. Nothing was farther from the truth. Carter is a wimp. George Bush is Dudley Do-Right.

George Bush is a gentleman, an athlete, a decorated WWII Navy pilot, and a former head of the Republican National Committee. He served in Congress and served previous presidents as a diplomat and a spy. He was a loyal vice president who won over the heart of Reagan by his understanding of governmental etiquette and diplomatic protocol after Reagan was shot. Not a wimp, but definitely a "golly gee whiz" type of guy who still opened doors for ladies and fixed his own plumbing. In New England we call them "Yankees."

After losing the now-prerequisite 1988 Iowa caucus to Senator Bob Dole, Vice President Bush was put on notice. He was not going to remain Reagan's lapdog and win the presidency. Bush was going to have to get down and dirty and say bad things about people, which was completely out of character. Republicans were not meant to speak ill of other Republicans, yet this was the eighties and just about anything went.

So the Bush camp hired Lee Atwater to be the campaign's pit bull and protect the springer spaniel candidate from the other junkyard dogs in politics. It worked. First they finished off Dole then moved on to the Democratic Party's nominee, Michael Dukakis, governor of Massachusetts.

I could write volumes on the incompetence of Michael Dukakis, but rather let us wander just a few feet down that garden path to make my point. He is from my hometown of Brookline. He was the little skin kicker who harassed my father on Election Day 1958 and threatened to file papers against him because he was wearing a campaign button too close to an election booth. When my family was tearing up the playing fields of Brookline, Dukakis was checking coats at the senior prom. Dukakis is the quintessential wimp.

When Dukakis became governor during a fiscally challenging period, he promised not to increase taxes and balance the budget. He did neither. He took public transportation to work. Down-to-earth guy? Nope, complete phony. He professed to be too frugal to take a car to his office in the Statehouse. For security reasons, his state-paid car and driver still had to follow the trolley car into Boston, and an additional trooper was required to ride on the trolley with him. Net event: a waste of time, a waste of money, a pure publicity stunt. Remind you of anyone? Another frugal governor who carried his own suitcase? Yup, Jimmy Carter, another wimp.

When Dukakis was not raising taxes, forming investigative committees, and sending the state police out to raise revenues by writing speeding tickets, he was spending most of his time pardoning and furloughing criminals. He even pardoned Sacco and Vanzetti for being anarchists, fifty years after they were electrocuted. He attempted to decommission statewide committees that actually worked well. He was so out of touch with Massachusetts, even his state police union turned on him, and he lost his renomination to fiscally conservative Democrat Ed King.

King, a former NFL player and successful executive, was not a gifted politician and made some rather poor appointments as governor. The *Boston Globe* was relentless in its attacks on King, and after four years, Massachusetts voters reinstated Dukakis as governor. What was unknown to the biased *Boston Globe*, and its readers, was that King returned Massachusetts to a fiscally happening place to work, live, and prosper. Unfortunately, it takes more than four years to turn an economy around, and when it did rebound, Dukakis was governor again and took all the credit for the "Massachusetts Miracle."

How anyone bought this guy's baloney is beyond me, but remember I'm from Massachusetts and voters love guys like this. Either way, he slowly eliminated his competition during the Democratic primaries and headed to the Democratic National Convention as the uncrowned nominee. When Dukakis's foreign policy experience was called into question, some campaign hack put a helmet on Dukakis and had him drive a rented tank. He looked like a little kid. The editorial cartoons were very amusing; one lampooned him as "Snoopy" driving the tank. There was much Dukakis was fearful of admitting or disclosing, but it was Bush's hired gun Lee Atwater's job to "tear the bark off" him.

When Kitty Dukakis married Michael Dukakis, he was already on his way in Massachusetts politics. She never felt she needed to mention that she was Jewish, had a first husband and son, or had a problem with alcohol and drugs. Lee Atwater's team began spreading rumors about

Kitty; that she was an ultraliberal radical who burned an American flag, was unfaithful, and was a substance abuser. *The New York Times* began investigating rumors of the candidate's mental health and requested he disclose his medical records. Dukakis declined. President Reagan, when asked about the topic, responded, "Look, I'm not going to pick on an invalid."

Atwater's team continued accusations about Dukakis's membership in the American Civil Liberties Union, his vetoing a law allowing schoolteachers to lead the class in the Pledge of Allegiance, his opposition of the death penalty, and his wife's religious affiliation. They also made career criminal Willie Horton a household name.

Willie Horton was a convicted Massachusetts murderer. He stabbed a seventeen-year-old gas station attendant to death during a robbery, even after the kid handed over the cash. Horton was sentenced to life in prison without the possibility of parole. Dukakis allowed him out of jail on a weekend furlough, and Horton never returned. Instead, Horton went to Maryland, where he robbed, stabbed, and pistol-whipped a bound man who was forced to watch Horton rape his fiancée, twice. Charming. Dukakis continues to defend the controversial program.

A moderator during a presidential debate asked Dukakis if Kitty were raped and murdered, would he change his opinion on the death penalty. Dukakis answered in the negative, with all the passion of being asked if he wanted a side order of fries. It cost him the election. Thank God.

When George H.W. Bush became president, he was the first sitting vice president to be elected president since Martin Van Buren in 1836. Bush traveled all over the world as Reagan's emissary and attended numerous funerals for heads of state, including three Soviet premiers. Bush was president when the body politic of the USSR died in the fall of 1989, but he declined to go to the Berlin Wall to spike the football.

Most thought he should go, for Kennedy and for Reagan, but Bush was a foreign relations aficionado and did not want to be the fist-pumping victor standing at Brandenburg gate. He understood defeated Germany's Versailles Syndrome, which led to strong nationalism and the rise of the Nazis. He was concerned the same might happen in one of the fifteen states of the former Union of Soviet Socialist Republics.

George Bush had better manners. After decades of confrontation and negotiation, why inflame a sensitive situation? Bush knew heroes do not boast. This is how capable George Bush was as our president. As a result, Bush was able to enjoy a robust relationship with the new Soviet leader, Mikhail Gorbachev.

As with most post-WWII presidents, Bush was also faced with the continued dangers in the Middle East. After Iraq's threats to Saudi Arabia's oil fields and the invasion of Kuwait, Bush lobbied the UN for action. With the UN's endorsement and authority, a US-led military coalition attacked and defeated Iraq, restoring peace to the region and rescuing Kuwait's sovereignty. Unfortunately, the UN did not authorize additional use of force, and coalition troops were forced to impotently witness Saddam Hussein's monsters murder his own people.

When American forces attacked, the battle was over before it really got started. An America company had sold the Iraqi Air Force its fighters, and when it was time to address the issue of an air strike, the CIA flicked a switch and decommissioned the entire fleet. Iraqi jet fighters never left the ground. Our next concern was the thousands of tanks in the Iraqi desert. They turned out to be of inferior quality and easily destroyed in tank warfare. The navy launched Patriot missiles into Iraq, rendering their Scud missiles useless. Furthermore, the country watched the successful sorties every night on television. It was a wild time. Soldiers were safer fighting in Iraq than driving the highways of America. Bush was a mighty powerful commander in chief.

Then there was the domestic war on drugs. Cocaine was entering the United States at an unprecedented volume. But it wasn't just Upper East Side stockbrokers snorting a little blow over the weekend. Chemists had doctored the drug into a crystallized form of cocaine, called "crack." George Bush surreally held up a bag of it on national television from the Oval Office and told the nation, "This is a bag of crack cocaine. It's as innocent looking as candy, but it's turning our cities into battle zones and it's murdering our children."

A devastatingly addictive and inexpensive drug, crack quickly found its way into the underbelly of America's cities, festering there until it became a national epidemic. Crime rates soared as inner-city minorities began peddling it, making huge profits and creating a criminal subculture that remains in existence today. Bush fought back as hard as he could, but the supply was so great that cocaine street value plummeted while its demand soared—hardly microeconomics.

US intelligence determined that General Manuel Noriega, a CIA-trained de facto leader of Panama, was trafficking South American drug cartels' product into the United States and laundering the huge profits through legitimate banking operations. Reagan had already advised US ally Noriega to knock it off and hold free elections, which were a joke. When Bush became president, Noriega was repeatedly warned, and again the election results were disputed. In the world theater, Panama is a pawn. After a number of failed attempts to bring stability to Panama, Bush sent in the Marines, apprehended Noriega, brought him to Miami, prosecuted him, and threw him in jail. Bush had the foreign policy knowledge and military expertise to take out the hemispherical tyrant and be done with him. Everyone, especially the Panamanians, agreed. Good riddance.

George Bush should have served two terms as president. He was the right guy for the job. As a foreign relations expert, there remained many hot beds of terrorism across the globe where his experience could have been an asset, but he made three fatal flaws in his reelection bid.

First, having been left with a huge deficit from Reagan's administration, Bush should have known that he would have to raise taxes to settle the account. Everyone in Washington knew there was a modicum of possibility that Bush would have to raise taxes, but he unequivocally declared he would not do so. When asked about taxes again, Bush firmly reiterated that he would not raise them. When questioned again about how he was going to solve the deficit, he insisted, "Read my lips, no new taxes." Bush raised taxes. To some, he lacked credibility; to others, he was a liar. His opponents lambasted him from every conceivable angle. Bush could not complain about their vicious attacks. It was his election four years earlier that lowered the bar on unscrupulous campaign tactics.

Second, Bush visited a grocery store in his vacation village in Maine. This is what regular fellas do. They go out and meet the locals, shoot the breeze, and act like one of the guys. George Bush even purchased a few sundries at the local store. When he got to the checkout counter, he not only couldn't believe the cost of a loaf of bread, but he was fascinated with the barcode scanner. Having been on the taxpayers' cuff for the past twelve years, he began to understand how out of touch he really was, and the nation agreed. Polls indicated it was time for him to get his credit cards back from the government and buy his own groceries.

Finally, during the presidential debates, he could not relate to basic questions from the audience. After bungling a simple question from what appeared to be a hardworking woman about the economy and jobs, he allowed a "used car sales-man" to steal his thunder and answer the question. Then Bush looked at his watch as if he had somewhere else to be or something better to do. Good-bye, George Bush. Hello, Bill Clinton.

Russian President Boris Yeltsin & Bill Clinton

White House Photograph

19

THE CLINTONS & CRIMES AGAINST REALITY

It is a well-established fact that at the conclusion of the Gulf War, President Bush had an 80 percent job approval rating. Who would imagine that two years later he would lose his reelection campaign with less than 38 percent of the popular vote? His opponent had focused on the weak economy rather than Bush's foreign policy accomplishments, and it worked.

Arkansas Governor William Jefferson "Slick Willie" Clinton was the windbag who was booed off the 1988 Democratic National Convention stage for laboring on too long about his dear friend Michael Dukakis. In 1992, Clinton ran for president as a "New Democrat," part of a group of centrists founded by the Democratic Leadership Council.

The New Democrats' philosophy was hatched from a think tank, and they based their agenda on the principles of personal and fiscal accountability and free trade, while still maintaining the fundamental liberal thesis of Progressivism. More closely aligned with the realism of a Truman-Kennedy style of open market policies rather than the far-left leanings of Keynesian economics, the New Democrats employed a "the third way" philosophy that resonated Jefferson's and Jackson's constitutional concepts of individual responsibility, a decentralized government, and balanced budgets.

The three main factors that aided Bill Clinton's success in the general election were the weak economy, Bush's capitulation on his promise that he would not raise taxes, and third-party "spoiler" candidate Ross Perot, who eroded 19 percent of the popular vote. Clinton attracted only 43 percent, hardly a mandate, but Bush lost the election.

There were also three character flaws of Bill Clinton that nearly cost him the election: the persistent rumors of adulterous behavior, allegations of being a draft dodger, and suspicion that he was a pathological liar. When questioned on each of these subjects, Slick Willie lived up to his moniker and slithered away without uttering a coherent response. The press could not get a straight answer from him about any of it, except in the form of a denial. The round-the-clock cable news programs thrived off his controversial personality and alleged sexual dalliances. After all, sex sells.

Forget the meaningful issues. To further illustrate the point that Clinton was neither fish nor fowl, in the quest to discover the true nature of his persona, the press asked if he ever smoked marijuana. Slick Willie replied he tried it, but he didn't inhale.

Guffaw. Who the hell admits to smoking pot, especially during the Woodstock era, and then denies catching a buzz? Slick Willie, that's who. That statement is completely illogical. For me, I wanted a fellow baby boomer to stand up to the press and announce, "Yeah, I smoked pot in college. I had a lot of fun playing Frisbee, not going to war, chasing girls, listening to good music, and getting stoned." But not Clinton. Instead, he lied, and for no good reason. Responses such as these remain curious and appear excessively contrived for a guy as smart as Bill Clinton. Was he lying for practice? Was he a pathological liar? And what exactly was he trying to pull over on us?

There is no debate that Bill Clinton is a shameless opportunist and a lovable scamp, but what truly makes him tick? One can only speculate that he was the guy in high school who brown-nosed the teachers, always got the good grades, and always got the girl, but no one really knew. As Oscar Wilde once wagged, "The only thing worse than being talked about is not being talked about." And talk they did.

Also nicknamed the "Comeback Kid," Clinton had won elections, lost elections, and won back elections during the ebbs and flows of his political career in Arkansas. Despite his visceral critics and personal shortcomings, Clinton remained the consummate politician; he was socially engaging, making those whom he was speaking with feel the center of his attention. He was also incredibly charming and remarkably intelligent. Clinton was a Rhodes scholar from Georgetown

University with a law degree from Yale, which is where he met and later married Hillary Rodham.

Hillary Rodham was a feminist who grew up Chicago and headed the Young Republicans at Wellesley College. She jumped ship to the Democrats after an unpleasant experience at the 1968 Republican National Convention. After Wellesley she matriculated to Yale Law School. During summers she interned at a liberal law firm in Oakland, California, and worked on the House Judiciary Committee preparing to impeach Richard Nixon. After graduation from Yale, she married Clinton, moved to Arkansas, and began plotting Slick Willie's political career. If there was ever a pair of political chameleons, it was the Clintons.

Bill Clinton stated during the presidential campaign that, if elected, Hillary would be a full partner in his administration, coining the slogan, "Buy one, get one free.'" Hillary was as controversial as her husband from the very beginning. Together they were known as "Billary," and the press loved every minute of it.

As the Clintons began to win primaries and draw the attention of the national press, Hillary was questioned on an Arkansas ethics and disclosure law, a bill manipulated by Slick Willie to exempt himself and his family from doing business with the state. The condescending Lady Macbeth of Little Rock responded, "I suppose I could have stayed home and baked cookies." An arrogant and dismissive defense for a legitimate question that simultaneously demeaned stay-at-home moms.

Later, when Bill Clinton was confronted with evidence of his adulterous affair with a cabaret singer, he denied everything and let his wife do his bidding for him. Hillary revitalized her husband's presidential hopes by responding to a *Sixty Minutes* question on his infidelity, stating, "I'm not sitting here, some little woman 'standing by her man' like Tammy Wynette. I'm sitting here because I love him and I respect him." The reference was a hit country-and-western song from 1968 that was originally ridiculed by feminists for perpetuating the role of pathetic wives trapped in emotionally abusive and adulterous marriages. Yet Hillary was doing just that, standing by her lying, cheating husband. Her life was imitating art. She might have been educated at one of the best colleges and universities in the nation, but now she was nothing more than hillbilly trailer trash.

Members of the national press were dually cautious and intrigued with the Clintons. They were the perfect yuppie "power couple": well educated, calculating, rigid, which made for great copy. Fellow Democrats were slow to show initial support of Bill Clinton, as his persona was perceived by some to be devilishly superficial and illegitimate. On Super Tuesday, Bill Clinton, the southerner governor, won big in the Florida and Texas primaries and became the Democratic Party's front-runner.

Along with his parallel prototype, Al Gore, as the vice presidential candidate, Clinton won the election to become our forty-second president. The Democrats took home all the marbles in 1992; they now controlled the House, the Senate, and the White House for the first time in sixteen years. "Happy Days Are Here Again"? It was still too soon to strike up the band.

Trouble with Hillary began immediately after inauguration. As the first wife of a president with a postgraduate degree, she was also the original first lady with an office in the West Wing. Hillary promptly garnered control of the White House travel department, fired seven long-serving, nonpolitical employees, and hired family and friends from Arkansas to run the office. When questioned why she would do such a thing, she lied. In fact she had ordered FBI files on the guy who ran the travel office, looking for a reason to dismiss him.

Vince Foster, her good friend and Little Rock law partner who was now deputy White House counsel, voiced concern. In response, the *Wall Street Journal* made inquiries into Foster's personal life and professional dealings with the Clintons. The result left him distressed and ambivalent of political life in Washington. One day he left his office, went for a walk in a federal park, and committed suicide.

Ignoring all of the intelligence and forensic agencies available to the Clinton administration, the White House put the United State Park Department in charge of investigating the gunshot suicide of its deputy counsel. Never in its two-hundred-year history had the Park Department investigated a murder or suicide. Suspicion swirled around Washington. Why would an apparently stable and competent attorney commit suicide? Was there a scandal? Were there illegal practices? Marital infidelity? It's the Clintons, after all. There had to be more to the story. But the press was stonewalled.

Hillary also recommended a former barroom bouncer and dirty trickster, Craig Livingstone, for the job as head of White House Office of Personnel Security. Livingstone requested the release of FBI files on Republicans for Hillary to peruse and was caught. Hillary was aware from her experience on the House committee during the Nixon impeachment process that the misuse of FBI files was not only illegal, but also a jailable offense. Livingstone was dismissed for being both underqualified for the job and for his involvement with the illegally obtained FBI files. Of course Hillary denied all knowledge of either. Off to a great start.

When the president appointed Hillary to administer the Task Force on National Health Care Reform, the Democratic Congress snubbed its nose at her. Congressional cooperation between the executive branch is controlled by the Oval Office, not the first lady. Clinton should never have put his wife in charge of such an effort. It proved immaturity and inexperience. Congress began to cast a questioning glare at the new president. It is nothing new for state governors who become presidents to feel like outsiders in Washington, because they are. Clinton had no political currency in Washington, and currying favor takes years of ass kissing. Bringing his wife into the mix on such an important piece of legislation went over like a fart in church. This was Washington, not Little Rock.

Clinton may have had illusions of being a Wilson or a Roosevelt, with a bevy of one-hundred-day legislation, or operating similar to LBJ, who could find financing for an ice cube factory in Anchorage if he needed to get a bill passed. But team Billary found that proper protocol and the power of persuasion in Washington was going to be more difficult than appeasing "Bubba," their personification of a southern, blue-collar, beer-drinking good old boy.

Then a Bubba from Arkansas came back to bite them right in their backsides. David Hale, a former Arkansas judge and banker, who was pleading guilty to defrauding the Small Business Administration—ugh—agreed to testify about a failed saving and loans executive and a former client of Hillary's, James McDougal. In an attempt to lessen his sentence, Hale alleged in US District Court that Governor Clinton pressured him into making an illegal loan to McDougal and the Whitewater Development Corporation, a real estate investment company in which the Clintons were investors. The Securities and Exchange Commission did convict McDougal and his wife, Susan, on Hale's testimony, but the Clintons were never prosecuted. Natch.

Questions continued to circulate about the Clintons, the McDougals, the failed S&L, and Whitewater. When the press inquired, the Clintons ignored them. When the press pushed harder, the Clintons pushed back harder. Whitewater became yet another national controversy and the catalyst for the appointment of a special prosecutor.

When the special prosecutor wanted to see the files on Whitewater Development Corporation, the Rose Law firm denied it had them. When it was discovered that the files had gone to the White House with Vince Foster, the special prosecutor requested them from the White House. It was determined that files on Whitewater had disappeared from Vince Foster's office after his death. When asked where they landed, the White House pleaded ignorance. No one seemed to know. The press and the prosecutor smelled a rat; was this the smoking gun of Vince Foster's suicide? What were the Clintons trying to hide? Again, there must be something these attorneys were trying to conceal. The files eventually and surprisingly appeared in the Clintons' private residence of the White House. To this day, no one knows or will admit how they got there. Even the Clintons. Curious.

Another Bubba, now playing the role of numerous Arkansas state troopers, alleged that Governor Clinton asked them to arrange sexual dalliances with women. Referring to themselves as "pimps," the state troopers discussed numerous predatory episodes of Governor Clinton's philandering, especially with state employees and one in particular named Paula. Her name was Paula Jones, and soon the special prosecutor and then the press would draw her into the Whitewater investigation. After all, sex sells.

Additionally, the *New York Times* asserted that Hillary had begun a part-time career in trading commodities futures while her husband was attorney general of Arkansas. She and Tyson Foods outside counsel Jim Blair parlayed $1,000 into over $100,000 in less than a year. It was suspected that Blair was running profitable trades through Hillary's illegal margin account to gain influence with her husband. The *Journal of Economics and Finance* economists investigated the odds of gaining a hundred-fold return in the cattle futures market during the period in question. Using a model that was stated to give the hypothetical investor the benefit of the doubt, they concluded that the odds of such a return happening were at best one in thirty-one trillion. The Chicago Mercantile Exchange investigated and determined that its margin rules had been violated and nothing else. Besides, the statue of limitations had expired. Another bullet dodged.

The press that was originally behind him was sensing an unpleasant pattern of deceitful practices permeating from Arkansas. We all began to wonder how much we knew about the Clintons after all and whether we had we been duped again by the sweet drawl of an unfamiliar southern governor.

In spite of it all, Clinton kept on pushing economic legislation. He believed he was taking the nation in a new direction. The Deficit Reduction Act of 1993 passed Congress without a

Republican vote, and Clinton signed it into law. The act cut taxes for fifteen million low-income families, made tax cuts available to 90 percent of small businesses, and raised taxes on the wealthiest 1.2 percent of taxpayers. Additionally, through the implementation of spending restraints, it mandated the budget be balanced over a number of years. It was accomplished, and the government had the first budget surplus in thirty years. It sparked the greatest peacetime expansion in the nation's history.

Clinton's first year as president was challenging. It seemed that there was a new scandal every week. It began with Travelgate, and now there was Filegate, Whitewatergate, and bimbos at the gate. Vince Foster was dead, his files were missing, Hillary was in the hamper, and there were problems getting a legally qualified woman without personal improprieties to become attorney general. Small stuff like that.

When Hillary worked on the House committee to impeach Nixon, she had sworn that the days of backroom politics were over and that women were on hand to make sure that Nixon's style of dirty tricks ceased to exist in politics. Seems to me she learned just enough to be dangerous.

Clinton did resolve a controversial campaign pledge regarding homosexuals in the military. With an edict known as "don't ask, don't tell," Clinton put the sensitive issue to rest. No one understood what it meant, but it was an end to a huge distraction for the new president. It also perfectly epitomized the ambiguity of the Clinton administration, another confusing concessionary concept, same as "I didn't inhale," and it placated few.

Starting with New Year's Day 1994, Clinton's second year as president began on a positive note. He signed in NAFTA, the North American Free Trade Agreement. He signed a crime package that included the death penalty for additional categories of criminals: drug lords, repeat violent offenders, and killers of federal agents. This was good stuff, yet the year would end with a thud.

The public disapproval ratings of Bill Clinton surged with continued distrust of Team Billary. In the House, Representative Newt Gingrich began the "Contract with America" and challenged the policies of the first New Democrat presidency. In the midterm elections, Gingrich and the Republicans beat the Democrats with a stick. There was a fifty-four-seat swing in the House and an eight-seat swing in the Senate, giving Republicans control of both chambers for the first time in forty years. This election became known as the Republican Revolution. Clinton was seriously marginalized and crestfallen.

Yet Bill Clinton is a megalomaniac. He hated that people did not like him or trust him, and he hated the fact that his presidency was going to be short-sheeted by a Republican Congress. He needed to find another way, a fourth way, to conduct business in Washington and return himself to a favorable spotlight. Remember there is nothing an opportunist will not do, so Clinton left the New Democrats at the door and reinvented himself as the white-stripe-down-the-middle-of-the-road president. He was willing to do whatever he had to do to win back the American people's respect and their votes; the ubiquitous Comeback Kid.

One of the major battles between the Republican House and the Democratic White House was the budget. Clinton and newly elected Speaker of the House Gingrich got into a budgetary game of chicken, and as a result, some government buildings were shuttered and nonessential federal employees' pay was held in abeyance. At the White House, the executive branch was forced to tolerate unpaid interns to assist in the daily activities of the West Wing. One of these interns was a twenty-one-year-old recent college graduate from California named Monica Lewinsky. A name that became a verb.

The budget battles were resolved with welfare reform and taxpayer relief acts, but in reality the balanced budget was the result of Gingrich's Contract with America. Yet Clinton, the opportunist, claimed responsibility for the surplus and waved his centrist flag in celebration. He seemed to be back in good stead with the American public. Maybe the Comeback kid could win reelection.

But first Bill Clinton needed to fund his 1996 reelection campaign. Slick Willie emulated his namesake, bank robber Slick Willie Sutton, and went to where the money was. Bill Clinton went to Wall Street not for advice or as a resource for administrative talent; he went to Wall Street for political donations.

By promising to reform the Glass-Steagall Act and to delay and derail legislation to regulate derivatives, Clinton's reelection fund was well financed by enormous donations from Wall Street executives. He also promised to emasculate the regulatory arm of the Securities and Exchange Commission. The investment firms, now with a presidential blessing, could do whatever they wanted without fear of consequence. Fellow southerners Jefferson and Jackson would have been so proud.

The Banking Act of 1933, aka the Glass–Steagall Act, and the Securities Acts of 1933 were passed during the Roosevelt administration as parallel regulation to correct the unbridled financial lending practices that caused the Great Depression. The Banking Act was also a decree to restore public faith in the United States banking system. These were imperatively important objectives of Roosevelt's recovery process.

Primarily, the Banking Act created the Federal Deposit Insurance Corporation to federally insure the funds of banks depositors. Additionally, it forbade commercial banks from making "risky" investments with depositors' funds. Risky investments included trading securities, underwriting securities, or making loans to institutions trading securities. Even officers of the banks were restricted from being affiliated with investment firms under a conflict-of-interest clause. The Securities Acts of 1933 and the creation of the Securities and Exchange

Commission would administer and regulate "risky" investments and trading operations. Banks were to be autonomous from Wall Street speculation. Together these acts were the yin and yang of the nation's sphere of capital and wealth.

The intricacies of Glass-Steagall have been debated many times since its inception. Congress attempted to reform it and presidents have challenged it, but the skeletal body remained firmly intact. That was, of course, until Bill Clinton and his cronies came to town and set it on fire.

Clinton's secretary of the treasury, Robert Rubin, the former head of investment firm Goldman Sachs, determined after very little investigatory evidence that the act was "out of synch with reality," and he took his case to Congress. The Gramm-Leach-Bliley Act, aka the Financial Services Modernization Act of 1999, was passed by Congress to justify the predated waiver given to the $76 billion merger of Traveler's Insurance and Citicorp. Rubin stated, "It is now time for the laws to reflect changes in the world's financial system." Yup, right after Citicorp appointed former president Gerald "Now It's My Turn" Ford to its board of directors to lobby the Republican aisles of Congress, while Clinton and Rubin worked their magic with the Democrats.

A casual observer might assume that the overhyped dot-com bubble of 2000 or the terrorist attacks in 2001 caused the near-collapse of the US markets nearly a decade later. Those who understand the toxic combination of Wall Street financiers and a morally corrupt Congress, blessed by the illicit policies of the Clinton White House, can elucidate the genesis the global economic disaster we find ourselves in today, while Wall Street continues to rake in billions.

The Wall Street fundraising was technically legal, but much of Bill Clinton and Al Gore's reelection fundraising was not. Al Gore attended illegal fund-raisers held by illegal foreign nationals at illegal sites to raise money for their campaign. The Justice Department could not find good reason to investigate, even after the illegal fund-raisers admitted the funds had been illegally obtained by illegal practices at illegal sites—but the funds were lawfully returned!

Some of the questionable sponsors of the fund-raisers were Asian bundlers for People's Republic of China who were given personal tours of the White House by Clinton. Check that, Asian gangsters and Red communist security agents were given access to the White House. One bundler referred to the admittance at the White House as similar to gaining entrance to a subway, by "putting coins in the turnstile." Eventually twenty-two individuals were convicted of fraud and funneling Asian funds into the Democratic National Committee and United States campaigns. Many were directly associated with Clinton and Gore.

It is also illegal to use government buildings for political fundraising. President Clinton and Vice President Al Gore used the White House for fundraising and freely admitted it.

They defended their actions by some imaginary sense of reality, stating they were candidates at the time of the fundraising and not elected officials. What? If they were not elected officials, who was running the country and what were they doing in the White House? Lanny Davis, special counsel to the president, not only admitted it was true but said that they held many more events for donors and political supporters at the White House than had been previously disclosed. But the 1996 election was over. We won, so don't worry about it.

This was also true with the Hollywood contributors. Over three hundred guests stayed in diplomatic bedroom suites within the private living quarters of the White House. Seats aboard Air Force One were sold to $100,000 contributors. When it was determined that former DNC head Ron Brown, now Clinton's secretary of commerce, was being investigated for selling seats on his air force jet on foreign trips, his jet mysteriously crashed in Croatia, and that put an end to that.

Putting the fund-raising aside, one legitimate concern for the American public was Clinton's lack of foreign policy experience. Clinton came into office as the first post-Cold War president and the first president never to wear a uniform since WWII. There also remained unanswered allegations about draft dodging, and the fact that he protested the Vietnam War as a student in England, which some found treasonous. Clinton became commander in chief when the United States was the sole superpower and globally respected by all but a few Islamic extremists.

During the 1992 general election, President Bush noted that, "My dog Millie knows more about foreign affairs than these two bozos", referring of course to Clinton and Gore.

So it was to no surprise that as commander in chief, Clinton haphazardly dispatched helicopters to Somalia to quell the brutalities of its civil war. Jimmy Carter could have advised the young president about the dangers of using military helicopters in deserts. Furthermore, the image of helicopters conjured up unpleasant nostalgic reminders of hovering Hueys in Vietnam.

This was a massive miscalculation by Clinton, and it went terribly wrong. Two Blackhawk helicopters crashed, and eighteen US troops were killed, their bodies desecrated, their remains dragged around town for the whole world to see in the hullabaloo of twenty-four-hour cable news portals. America had tried to forget images such as these. We had hoped to move forward from the realities of war and from playing the role of global policemen, but we had not.

Clinton, like Johnson and Carter, was in over his head. What else was new? Rookie presidents always make a few military mistakes. This misstep was a wake-up call to remind the Clinton administration of the potential reality that any minor military engagement could flare up into a colossal firestorm such as Vietnam. Bill Clinton learned the lesson that African civil wars are costly, so avoid them at all costs. Later, during the Rwandan civil war, Clinton refused to send military aid, and as a result over half a million Rwandans were murdered. No one in his administration had an appetite for war, especially the baby boomers of the Vietnam era. No more Vietnams, no matter what.

The fact remains that US citizens and soldiers were attacked in at least five incidents during Clinton's presidency. The first was the World Trade Center attacks that came just as he assumed office in 1993. In response, he talked tough but did nothing. When US intelligence determined that it was Islamic terrorists, he said nothing. He went on MTV, and stated that the bombing was done by people who "did something really stupid." Yeah, they killed six people and injured thousands, and Clinton did nothing. Our new commander in chief, what a standard bearer.

When the US Air Force housing complex Khobar Towers in Saudi Arabia was attacked in 1996 and nineteen US service-men were killed, he said, "The explosion appears to be the work of terrorists. The cowards who committed this murderous act must not go unpunished. America takes care of its own." There were over one hundred intelligence reports indicating a pending attack. He did nothing to prevent the attack and nothing in response. Nothing, nada, zilch.

When US Embassies in Tanzania and Kenya were bombed and twelve US citizens were killed, some Marines, some CIA operatives, Clinton's response was to bomb a pharmaceutical factory in Sudan. Although it was something, it was done right after he admitted committing perjury. His critics speculated it was Clinton trying to appear "presidential" or a "wag the dog" exercise. However ineffectual, he did do something, but he did not kill the henchman, Osama bin Laden.

Then the *USS Cole*, a Navy destroyer cruising off Yemen, was attacked by Osama bin Laden's al-Qaeda in 2000. Again Clinton did nothing. This is a US warship attacked by terrorists, and seventeen US sailors were killed. Nothing. Clinton treated all attacks, except the embassy bombings, as if they were a law-enforcement issue, not a military matter. According to the future 9/11 report, even bin Laden, the hostile terrorist provocateur, complained he was frustrated that he could not lure Clinton into a military response.

But it was Clinton's inability to deal with the growing Islamic lunatics that caused the nation the greatest tragedy: September 11, 2001. "The biggest mistake of my presidency," Clinton admitted in retrospect, "was not going after Osama bin Laden."

This is what you get when you hire a womanizing, draft-dodging politician to manage the military—nothing. His political pollster, Dick Morris, alleges in his book on Clinton, "He had almost an allergy to using people in uniform. He was terrified of incurring casualties; the lessons of Vietnam were ingrained far too deeply in him. He lacked a faith that it would work, and I think he was constantly fearful of reprisals." Marvelous.

So here we have a president and first lady who have been under investigation by a special prosecutor since the beginning of their eight-year administration. They misused their positions of power for every reason imaginable and denied all charges brought against them. In some cases they admitted to errors but arrogantly implied, "So what, what are you going to do about it?" And they were right; there was no smoking gun to any of the accusations of their illegal activities. They were gifted grafters, but even whores have an Achilles' heel.

If the United States in the 1980s was all about conspicuous consumption, then the 1990s was all about recovery from the prior decade of decadence. Membership in nonjudgmental twelve-step groups was now openly acknowledged and socially acceptable. Recovery from addictions and the phrases from its teachings seeped into the society's vernacular. A "Friend of Bill" is a discreet reference to a fellow member of Alcoholics Anonymous, via its founder, Bill Wilson. Slick Willie took it as his own, designating his closest associates as FOBs. I am sure Bill Clinton was familiar with the self-help recovery programs, as his stepfather was a violent alcoholic, his mother a notorious gambler, and his half brother served time in jail for cocaine conviction. As a sex addict, he should also know something about the program's steps of taking a moral inventory and making amends, but he did neither.

Even though Clinton was a married man, a father, a lawyer, an elected leader in a position of ultimate authority, the highest office in the land—an office that requires an oath to "honor, protect, and defend the Constitution"—Clinton remained a sexual reprobate.

When Clinton was accused of having sex with White House intern Monica Lewinsky, he lied about it to his family, his friends, his administration, his Cabinet, to Congress, and to the United States of America. He also violated the laws of the Constitution that he swore to uphold, and he played right into the hands of his critics. He was finally exposed as the lying, cheating, manipulating horn dog we had all been warned about, and he continued to deny all of it.

During a White House press conference, with the first lady and the vice president standing at his side, Clinton discussed the future of the nation's children and after-school activities. "Every child needs someplace to go after school," he said. "With after-school programs, we cannot only keep our kids healthy and happy and safe, we can help to teach them to say no to drugs, alcohol, and crime, yes to reading, sports, and computers."

Curious he never mentioned anything about kids saying no to sex or protecting young girls from lecherous older men. At the end of the press conference, Slick Willie wagged his finger at us, and with all of his self-righteous indignation, repeated the bald-faced lie of not having sex with "that woman," Monica Lewinsky. At the conclusion of his deceit, his brazen simian wife clapped her hands as he led the triumvirate from the photo op.

The next day, the president, without conscience, fed his critics and dispatched Hillary to New York City to be interviewed on national television and encouraged her to lie for him. She espoused a paranoid and delusional concept that in 1998 America there existed a vast right-wing conspiracy of Bill Clinton haters who planted a bimbo in the Oval Office and arranged for her to have sex with the president, without his knowledge or that of the Secret Service. What a coup!

As New York Time columnist Maureen Dowd scribed, "Hillary Clinton knows her husband is a hound dog. She knew it before she married him. But they have their deal. He supported her when she messed up on Whitewater and health care. So if the presidency hinges on 'he said, she said,' the first lady won't hesitate to supervise the vivisection of the former intern. The feminist icon in the White House doesn't flinch at smearing these women, even when she suspects they're telling the truth, because she feels they're instruments of a conspiracy. It may turn out that there are right-wing troublemakers involved here, but when Mrs. Clinton uses apocalyptic language she's just changing the subject."

The National Organization for Women, or NOW, "Is dedicated to making legal, political, social, and economic change in our society in order to achieve our goal, which is to eliminate sexism and end all oppression." To me, it is profoundly interesting that NOW, whether with or without Hillary's approval, did not come out and make a public statement, pro or con, about this salacious string of events. Crickets.

One would assume that any organization seeking to "eliminate sexism" or promote feminism and/or equality would view the Lewinsky saga as *the* formidable case study: A successful and powerful older man meets a young, impressionable woman in the workplace. In this particular case, she is obviously politically or financially connected to this older man, as not everyone can get Secret Service clearance at his place of work, especially to be alone with him in his office. So he knows she is a team player.

Something happens, they flirt, they giggle, he shows her around "the best home court advantage in the world," and they go into his private study, where he seduces her. She provides oral sex, and he dismisses her. This happens frequently and then his wife comes home, or he has a crisis and he can't see the young girl as often. The sex-starved debutante gets pissed, calls a friend to complain about her love interest, and schemes to get even. An attorney is contacted; only this attorney is a federally funded special prosecutor investigating the older man for unethical behavior. The special prosecutor immediately begins another tangent to the ongoing investigation.

But not a word from NOW. If this happened in a private corner office of a *Fortune* 500 company, there would be lawsuits galore. But this happened in a public office with a man elected and compensated by taxpayers' dollars. Never mind that he is the leader of the free world, married to an avowed feminist, and NOW has nothing to say? They have plenty to say about elected officials and candidates' views on abortion, but nothing to say about the casting couch? As my friend Ralph

Donabed quipped, "This proves that all they really care about is being able to kill their babies."

Kenneth Starr replaced Robert Fisk as independent counsel (formerly known as special prosecutor) in summer 1994 to investigate Clinton's dealings with Whitewater. With the approval of Clinton Attorney General Janet Reno (yup, they finally found a qualified woman for the job), Starr began to expand his investigation into similar allegations of abuse and mistruths by the Clinton White House. He was now investigating the firing of the White House travel agents, the illegal use of FBI files, Vince Foster's suicide, and the sexual harassment suit by Paula Jones, whom Clinton harassed for oral sex when she was an Arkansas state employee.

Now Starr reached out to Linda Tripp, the Pentagon employee who had befriended Monica Lewinsky and taped their telephone discussions regarding oral sex with Slick Willie in the Oval Office.

Clinton was questioned by Paula Jones's attorney about Lewinsky, and you won't believe it—he lied, under oath. Not once or twice, but many times. He then went on television and lied. He lied so much, he forgot his lies. The prosecutors now had him dead to rights; he was a proven liar and perjurer. One would think that after witnessing the Nixon resignation, Clinton would have embraced his predecessor, George Washington, who it is said, "I cannot tell a lie."

Even after his pollsters told him that the nation would forgive a sinner but not a liar, he kept on lying. He attempted to weasel his way out of a confession by arguing over the meaning of the two-letter word is. This is a Rhodes scholar, a Yale Law School graduate, the former attorney general of Arkansas, now the president of the United States, and he insidiously lies about lying under oath. Finally Monica produced a semen-stained blue dress, and he could lie no longer. We had his DNA. All was true. He had to admit he was a philandering liar, not just to his country, but also to Hillary.

What trained liars forget is eventually the truth comes out. It cost the United States over $40 million to get Slick Willie to admit he was a horn dog. He hid behind religious leaders whom he called to the White House to advise him. They were all there, every size color and shape. Even Rev. Jesse Jackson was there with his mistress carrying his illegitimate child, as water seeks it own level.

"Clinton lied. A man might forget where he parks or where he lives, but he never forgets oral sex, no matter how bad it is," reminded Barbara Bush.

The Senate absolved Clinton, who was only the second president to be impeached by Congress. He was allowed to remain as president for the next two years, but his reputation was as stained as Monica's dress. Bill Clinton promised as president that his would be the "most ethical administration in the history of the country." Nothing could have been further from the truth, but then again, it depends what the truth really is.

Amazingly the people of America and the world forgave him. How they could, I will never know. He was forced to relinquish his law license for five years and agreed to pay off Paula Jones, and that was it. I am sure he had enormous legal bills, but no need to worry; he could just hold some more fund-raisers. Since he was no longer eligible to run for president and raise campaign funds, he exploited his last executive power: He sold presidential pardons to criminals and terrorists. He even pardoned his druggie brother. In all there were thirty-nine commutations and one hundred and fifty presidential pardons.

One of the last things he did before leaving 1600 Pennsylvania Avenue was pardon Susan McDougal for keeping her mouth shut and going to jail. She may have sat in jail for eighteen months, but she was alive. There is a documented trail of Clinton betrayers who ended up dead either from a suicidal gunshot or a plane crash.

Hillary needed something to do after being first lady. She tore a page out of Bobby Kennedy's playbook and ran for United States senator from New York. She wore a Yankees hat, claiming she was a lifelong Yankees fan. When asked if she could name the players with retired numbers, she could not hear the questions. I am a Red Sox fan, and even I can name them.

Hillary was elected and the Clintons moved to New York, but before they left the White House, in the middle of his pardons-for-sale period, they threw themselves a bridal shower and asked a few friends for china, crystal, and silver service for their new house in New York. Hillary ethically choreographed the receipt of the gifts to fall perfectly between leaving the White House and entering the Senate.

Seems they did not have any place settings of their own. When they got married, they had either no money or any friends, I guess, but they had plenty of both now. Then they looted the White House for a few furnishings. They got caught for that and had to return them to the American people. What a shame, or a sham. It is up to you to decide.

I met the guy a few times, once at my friend JFK Jr.'s funeral Mass. He came in and shook the hands of all the pallbearers, but I could not look him in the eye. The next time was at the White House on Saint Patrick's Day 2000. I was awash with emotion at being in the one-time home of my recently departed friend and thought it only apropos in his memory to do the right thing and to shake Clinton's hand in the receiving line.

I have to say: He does have a fantastic handshake and an overwhelming aura. I am not sure if I was groped, but I was captivated by him. It remains only unimaginable what he could have accomplished if he had not lied and instead had honored the truth, kept his pants zipped, and lived up to his marriage vows and presidential oath.

20

THE BATTLE OF THE
BABY BOOMERS

The presidential election of 2000 will be remembered as
one of the greatest debacles in modern United States politics.
We have endured close elections going back to the founding
of the republic, rife with accusations of corrupt bargains, adulterous relations, bigamy, illegitimate children, voter fraud, and
payoffs. All have weakened the integrity our extraordinary election process, but this is bare-knuckled politics, and it appears
the nation usually ends up with the best man for the job. What
is so disappointing about this election was Al Gore's childish
behavior deepened the troughs of bipartisan politics to an all-
time low, one we are still attempting, unsuccessfully, to backfill
three election cycles later.

Because Gore was defeated, angry liberals claimed George
W. Bush stole the election, and the wily press gave them a bull-
horn. Bush was elected; he did not steal anything. I am all for
the press keeping any president's feet to the fire, but what was
reported about Bush Jr. after the 2000 election is regretful, at
any level of civility.

Al Gore was vice president for two terms. We all knew him. We just liked him a little less than Bush as our next president. Gore had the benefit of raising long-term campaign financing from a position of power, the White House. He also had a sitting president to help him get elected, but Gore wanted to win this election on his own and avoided the litany of scandals associated with the Clinton administration. It's too bad, because the relationship worked as an asset for Hillary in New York, so Gore cannot blame Clinton. Gore has to assume responsibility; he lost the election.

Gore conceded the election to Bush, and then reneged. He took his little hanging chads all the way to the Supreme Court because he did not like the final tallying. This is not the character of a man I want running the country. The historical odds were against him winning the election; George Bush Sr. was the first sitting vice president to be elected president since 1836. Furthermore, the founding fathers had worked diligently to prevent such confusion in presidential elections. This is why presidents are elected by the Electoral College and not the popular vote, to avoid the "tyranny of the masses."

Allowing these accusations to continue for a month, dragging the stock market and the economy down with it, was not in the best interest of the country. To file suit in the Supreme Court was insult to injury. This elitist arrogance of entitlement was what cost Gore the election. Furthermore, by driving a wedge of partisanship in the House of Representatives, after it had just impeached your administrative colleague, propagated political party rancor. Neither was it a good idea to drum up animosity in his former haunts of the Senate chamber, after it had just absolved the impeached Clinton. Even Tricky Dick had enough class to take it like a man. The New Democrats who came to Washington claiming to do good things left it in shambles.

Granted, George W. Bush was not our most articulate president, but I do not believe there is an unpatriotic bone his body. He never blamed Clinton and Gore for 9/11. He took what transpired during his presidency like a man and reacted like a commander in chief should. For four years Bush was plagued by the conspiratorial rants of the liberals of stealing the 2000 election, lying to the world to instigate the wars on terror, and orchestrating the events 9/11 as an inside job. Hello, the lunatic left, and thanks to the press for perpetuating such utter nonsense and making it part of our daily lives.

In response, the Democratic National Convention came to Boston in 2004 and nominated our own junior senator, John F. Kerry, to be Bush Jr.'s opponent. To have the convention arrive in Boston was an amazing experience for me. I witnessed things I never thought possible for little old Beantown. Thousands of leading Democrats showed up, global celebrities appeared, world news organizations arrived with their satellite dishes, and the ominous security forces patrolled our streets.

This was the first political convention since the 9/11 attacks, so security was heightened. There was this strange presence of tactical responders carrying machine guns but no name tags or designating patches, nothing. They had a menacing appearance similar to masked Ninja warriors, dressed in black, wearing dark sunglasses, and with pants tucked into their paratrooper boots. Evidence of global terrorism in America was now walking the streets of historic Boston. It was sobering evidence of how much things had changed in America.

The mayor of Boston asked daily commuters to stay home during convention week, so the usually teeming streets were devoid of pedestrians and automobiles, giving the city the surreal appearance of a *Twilight Zone* episode. Miles away in suburbia, closed-circuit televisions were set up at traffic intersections, encircling the city. The Coast Guard patrolled Boston Harbor. Logan Airport was closed to private and non-commercial flights. This was serious stuff, and the convention was serious business. I was given a Secret Service pass and transported into the convention center on a bus that passed over a security ramp that bookended the transport and held it in abeyance until it was thoroughly inspected. Pretty weird stuff.

John Forbes Kerry had been breaking onto the political scene in Boston since he was a college student. As a volunteer in Teddy Kennedy's first Senate race in 1962, he began dating the half sister of first lady Jacqueline Kennedy and, like Clinton, met his idol, the real JFK, with whom he shared a monogram. After finishing Yale, Kerry entered the navy as an officer.

Kerry piloted a small patrol craft in Vietnam called a swift boat. Because of acts of bravery and battle injuries, Kerry was awarded a Silver Star, a Bronze Star, and the three Purple Hearts, the latter of which earned him a ticket stateside. After an honorable discharge, Kerry took up the cause célèbre of "Vietnam veterans against the war."

Due in part to his unusual demeanor and Ivy League eloquence, Kerry testified at congressional hearings claiming to have witnessed and participated in wartime atrocities. The following day Kerry joined fellow veterans, before the press, in throwing their medals on the steps of Congress in protest of US policy in Vietnam. Kerry continued to voice his opposition to the war on national television, usually dressed in fatigues.

Kerry returned to Massachusetts, got married, and had two children. He also ran for Congress. He lost and went to law school and later worked as a district attorney. Kerry then successfully ran for lieutenant governor on the Dukakis ticket. When Senator Paul Tsongas retired from the Senate for cancer-related health issues, the now-divorced Kerry ran for his seat and campaigned as a decorated war veteran, which caused some to pause.

Veterans began to question why Kerry would continue to boast of having earned medals of distinction in wartime if he had denounced and discarded them on the steps of Congress. Then it came out that he was actually displaying these medals in his home. When the press inquired about the allegations,

Kerry admitted the medals he threw at Congress belonged to someone else and his actions were merely a publicity stunt for implied effect, rather than his true convictions regarding his military record in the war.

Kerry won the election in spite of Ronald Reagan's reelection landslide, stating that the people of Massachusetts "emphatically reject the politics of selfishness and the notion that women must be treated as second-class citizens."

So now in Massachusetts we had two divorced and very single senators who kept a close eye on those second-class citizens. During the Reagan years, Kerry and Kennedy spent most of their leisure time in pursuit of young women and locating a new breed of supporters to fund their campaign chests and the DNC. Kerry was maintaining such a frugal existence, he slept on the couches of his associates' apartments in Washington rather than renting his own. His fund-raisers plotted to locate a revenue stream for Kerry to support his lifestyle.

The two playboy senators earned a few nicknames around town due to their extensive social calendars, but after the 1991 Palm Beach Easter weekend incident that put Teddy Kennedy's frat house antics back on the front page, the party tents were decamped and the two divorced Catholic senators cautiously returned to the covenants of marital bliss with second wives.

Kerry's new wife, Teresa Heinz, is the philanthropic widow of the late Republican Senator John Heinz from Pennsylvania.

The multimillionairess bought Kerry a prestigious home in Louisburg Square in Boston. The same Louisburg Square in which Mayor James Michael Curley would hold political orations early Sunday mornings to antagonize Boston's Brahmins. With the benefit of Heinz 57 wealth, Democrat Kerry was finally a legitimate homeowner and now full established to enjoy the private-jet existence he was previously denied by his ancestor's poorly financed trust funds and his parsimonious government salary.

After witnessing the debacle of fellow baby boomers Clinton and Gore's administration and with the availability of the Heinz ketchup fortune, Kerry began to clean himself up for a run at national office. He hired the best plastic surgeons, bought the most expensive suits, surrounded himself with Kennedy's surplus fund-raisers, and began his quest for the White House.

Kerry hit the campaign trail in his brand-new regular-guy barn jacket and took on a handful of fellow Democrats to get an early lead as the favorite. He also took on Bush Jr.'s wars on terrorism.

Although the Senate Foreign Affairs Committee member actually supported the war on Iraq, as a presidential candidate, he was now dead set against it. Kerry claimed Bush Jr. told him a lie. "When the president of the United States looks at you and tells you something, there should be some trust.", Kerry stated. I guess he forgot about Monica and his previous statement, "I will be voting to give the president of the United

States the authority to use force, if necessary, to disarm Saddam Hussein because I believe that a deadly arsenal of weapons of mass destruction in his hands is a real and grave threat to our security."

Kerry attempted to convince the national audience of voters that not only was he an honored veteran with wartime experience and medals to prove it, he was also more capable to serve as commander in chief than Bush Jr. Kerry's delivery smacked of insincerity and invalidity, and his fellow crewmen rejected the portrayal, declaring him "unfit to serve."

Swift boat veterans and former POWs formed a coalition of nonbelievers who questioned Kerry's patriotism, the accuracy of his recollections, and "willful distortion of the conduct" of fellow American servicemen during the war. After all, boots were on the ground in Afghanistan and Iraq.

There seemed to be an incongruous pattern about Kerry's recollection of his Vietnam War experience, his Senate voting record, and his previous comments on Iraq. Kerry began to flip and then flop, like a freshly caught cod. His infamous quote concerning the funding of troops in 2003 and then denying it in 2004 was, "I actually did vote for the $87 billion before I voted against it." He later dismissed the statement as an "inarticulate moment," but a litany of recanted facts began to emerge as the convention drew closer. A letter he co-wrote with fellow Democratic senators to President Clinton in 1998 appeared.

"We urge you, after consulting with Congress, and consistent with the US Constitution and Laws, to take necessary actions, (including, if appropriate, air and missile strikes on suspect Iraqi sites) to respond effectively to the threat posed by Iraq's refusal to end its weapons of mass destruction programs."

It is curious to me that with all the global intelligence available to the Clinton administration, Al Gore never broached the subject of terrorism or its threats to America during the 2000 election, as this election was all about preventing terrorism.

One of the DNC's events that week in Boston was a trip to Fenway Park. John Kerry showed up and was booed by local Red Sox fans. Later at a dinner, I was cornered by a member of the press who asked me about the public's reaction to Kerry. About a dozen sets of eyes were upon me. I attempted to explain, off the record.

First and foremost, I explained that I had contributed financially to Kerry's Senate campaign, and in Kerry's defense he had one of the most difficult jobs in the country from a constituency point of view. Teddy Kennedy ran the most influential constituency office in the country, if not the world. The fact is that Teddy Kennedy was not just our senator; we shared him with the nation, with the world. He was like the senator of the United States. If a constituent had an issue with a family member anywhere in the world, Lebanon,

Israel, China, or Peru, and that constituent needed assistance with the relative's well-being, the person called Kennedy's office before any other. In Massachusetts, Kerry was lost in Kennedy's shadow, but he deserved to be. When I made political donations to Teddy Kennedy, he sent me a personalized note thanking me. When I made contributions to Kerry, I never heard a word.

If Kerry kept his mouth shut and showed up for a few events each year and for reelection every six years, he could then jet off to Senator Heinz's ski house in Idaho, and no one would care. But Kerry wanted to be president. The locals were never really impressed with him and disliked his elitist Ivy League aloofness and his ever-evolving facial features. He is really sort of resented, but this is Massachusetts, and many things are tolerated and overlooked when you are a Democrat.

The press, as usual, put Kerry under the microscope. There is always more to the story when a politician begins to flip-flop. The press discovered that Kerry's implied Irish heritage was in fact false, and he had never made any attempt to correct the inaccuracy. Kerry was raised Catholic, but outside of his mother's Puritan roots in Massachusetts, his father's heritage was Austrian Jewish. It seems Kerry's paternal grandparents indiscriminately pointed to a spot in an atlas for their new surname in the Unites States, and his grandmother's finger landed on County Kerry, in southwestern Ireland. In Irish Catholic Democratic Massachusetts, why not let sleeping lies lie?

254

The Democratic National Convention in Boston was the highpoint of Teddy Kennedy's public career. He was the host, the master of ceremonies, and conductor of the Boston Symphony. He was having a ball. Kerry? He showed up to nomination night at the convention saluting the audience, stating, "I'm John Kerry, and I'm reporting for duty!"

Idiotic. Who were his handlers? He brought his questionable military career and the war back into the spotlight and gave validity to the Swift Vets and POWs for Truth, who then nailed the nominee to the barn door and set it on fire with vicious political ads at Kerry's expense. It only made Bush Jr. look more presidential.

There were other miscalculations. His wife told a member of the press to "shove it." Charming—a foreign-born woman, potentially the first lady, telling off the press in a less than ladylike manner. But the epitome of bad handling was the footage of Kerry windsurfing off Nantucket.

Whoever put Kerry on a windsurfing board and gave the press access was probably the same dolt who put the helmet on Dukakis and told him to drive the tank. Now the opposition had footage of a solitary windsurfer flip-flopping 180-degree turns in the trendy winds off the coast of tony Nantucket. Where was the down-to-earth guy in the barn jacket?

Two other elements caused Kerry's demise in the general election against the "worst president ever": the most liberal voting record in the Senate and selecting John "Help Is on the Way" Edwards as his running mate. As courtroom events have unfolded, it's become clear there is a special place in hell for cads like John Edwards. But the election was another squeaker for the second pair of baby boomers, and even though Kerry was approached about voter tampering in Ohio, he had enough class to not go looking for hanging chads.

There was one speaker at the convention who captured my attention. I did not recognize him until someone in my group said that was Barack Obama and he was going to be the first black president. I liked the sound of his name, so I stopped and listened.

He looked into the cameras on his right, his head oscillating to the left, then from left to right, stopping in the center, looking up, looking down toward the floor. It was obvious he was a Madison Avenue product, the African-American politician from the Illinois State Senate. First black president from Chicago, huh? That's what you said about Mel Reynolds, and he's in jail. Well, I was wrong again, but in the end, I was also very right.

21

THE LEGACY

There are all kinds of hell. In Dante's *Inferno*, he writes of the nine circles of hell, some of which have been touched upon in previous chapters. Other definitions of hell cannot aptly describe the horrors of such a dimension, as the human mind cannot conceive of infinite concepts. But basically hell is an evil netherworld where the cruel continue to live in a fiery existence among fallen angels and sinister demons. I know there is a living hell for people with mental illness, poverty, hunger, and addiction. I know that it is a curse to direct others there, and I know it is not a place I want to visit, even for an hour. But I also know that I could never endeavor to comprehend the six years of living hell that Captain John McCain endured as a guest at the Hanoi Hilton.

How anyone could vote against such a proud and distinguished naval officer for commander in chief, especially during a time of two wars in the Middle East, is beyond me. I was born in one of two years that are exempt from registering with the Selective Service System. The Vietnam War and the draft were over by the time I was old enough to vote. I know friends of my family who served in Vietnam. Some came home normal, some not so normal, and in the case of Dennis Reardon, he did not come home at all.

The treatment of returning Vietnam veterans was a travesty. We only witnessed the war on television what they personally endured. Still it is impossible to appreciate what they went through, and when they wanted to talk about it, no one ever really wanted to listen. Protestors spit on them and called them baby killers. These 18-year-old kids were drafted by their president to bring honor to previous veterans who defended our country. There were officers who anticipated serving in some capacity, and there were those who enlisted to fight for their country. I doubt if anyone of them did it for the pay; rather it was for the honor.

I can honestly express that I am pleased not to have served in Vietnam, but I'm proud of those who did. When I learned of what the POW actually suffered at the hands of the North Vietnamese, whether written in a book or depicted in a troubling film such as *The Deer Hunter*, I have to state that these men are heroes. There is no other way to describe them or their sacrifice. Knowing what I know now, I would follow John McCain into a barroom brawl, a street rumble between the Jets and the Sharks, the jungles of Southeast Asia, or the deserts of the Middle East, as well as up the stairs of the Capitol to watch him take the oath as president of the United States. I trust him.

It is obvious that in 2008, the country had grown fatigued of the Bush family's legacy of wars in the Middle East, and the eight years of deceit by the Clintons in between, but no one will ever convince me that in 2008 Barack Obama was qualified to be president.

This skinny, grinning, oscillating, smooth-talking dude is younger than me. He was the after thought replacement for the baby boomer fiasco of Clinton and Bush Jr. I did not think he offered much practical application or experience to lead the country, but the rest of the country sure did. It is not that I do not like him; I just do not trust him.

I have been around politics long enough to know that there are kingmakers; there are taciturn behind-the-scene-operators, wealthy philanthropists who promote their causes through effective politicians and unholy sycophantic lobbyists.

I also know there are packs of yapping dogs, gofers who will do or say just about anything to hang around the auspices of powerful political decisions. Campaigns are the perfect breeding ground for these political junkies. They usually work for impecunious pay and remain firmly convinced they are indispensable to the candidate or the staff. When they find out that they are not, they usually become political strategists or shrill commentators on Sunday morning talk shows.

I am quite certain that Barack Obama was a prepackaged minority version of JFK and promoted as such by the last reigning knight in the court of Camelot, Teddy Kennedy. The

Democrats had been struggling for a suitable presidential candidate for some time. Few had the longevity or seniority to go as deep as Teddy Kennedy; he had been around for nearly fifty years. It were as if a Wilsonian Democrat were alive and pulling the political strings of the party for JFK in 1960. It was also the 1968 prophesy of Bobby Kennedy that a Negro would be on the ballot in forty years.[15]

Teddy Kennedy worked on his brothers' 1960 and 1968 campaigns. He was elected to the Senate in between with a little financial help from his family and the adoring voters of Massachusetts, who never stopped reelecting him. After his brothers' deaths, Teddy stayed in the Senate and, with the influence of family members, decided that his 1980 presidential campaign would remain his singular attempt to reside at 1600 Pennsylvania Avenue.

What Kennedy had never been able to achieve was to appoint a successor, someone who would champion the causes he referred to at the conclusion of his presidential bid at the 1980 Democratic National Convention. Those causes, which remained incredibly worthy and meaningful, now seemed somewhat fatigued and obsolete. They needed a little modernizing. It was time for Teddy to use the same kind of clandestine maneuvering as he did when he slid the Immigration and Naturalization Act of 1965 by us, telling us everything was going to be all right, and he served Barack Obama to the country on a silver platter.

---

15 Washington Post, 5/27/1968.

Teddy Kennedy could host the convention in Boston, and he could assist his senatorial sidekick Kerry with guidance and political associations, but it was up to Kerry to get the votes necessary to be elected. Teddy Kennedy also knew that if he could get Barack Obama on the dais to speak, he could get him elected to the Senate, and they would take it from there if Kerry failed to win in 2004. Well, Obama did get on the stage, and he did win his Senate election and did get on the presidential ballot four years later. It is credible: Kennedy's father financially assisted the organization that sponsored Obama's father. Maybe this was the evidence of the inside job that gets the conspiracy fanatics up in arms.

When a self-effacing Obama asked Teddy Kennedy about his dearth of a legislative record and lack of practical political experience, Teddy counseled him that this was precisely the reason to run in 2008. With no sustainable record to attack, à la John Kerry, the press and his opponents could not hold him to any position or expertise on any matter. I know it sounds ludicrous but this strategy made perfect sense to Teddy Kennedy, and it worked.

I believe that if John F. Kennedy Jr., the true heir to the Camelot throne, had lived he would have beaten out Hillary Clinton's run for the US Senate from New York and would probably be on the national ticket in 2008. But piloting his plane on a hazy summer night eliminated that possibility. I believe that was Teddy's motivation: Barack was the only suitable substitute for John. Teddy was even able to convince reclusive Caroline to come out and politic for Obama, comparing him to her father, stating, "I feel that same excitement now." She was three years old when her father ran for president.

It was a perfect Kennedy strategy that sent Obama abroad to the Middle East and Europe to gain international credibility during his presidential campaign. It made perfect sense to hire Joe Biden, a true insider of Washington and fellow senator, as a vice presidential candidate, despite Obama claiming he wanted someone who had not been around the Beltway most of his life. Biden was first elected to the Senate when Nixon was president.

It was also perfect timing for campaign fund-raising. Obama had tapped into Al Gore's Internet and raised an astronomical amount of money. Obama was young, cool, hip, and a minority. It was the perfect storm.

It did not matter what Bill Clinton wanted or Hillary wanted. They were not going to get it. Teddy Kennedy held the presidential baton up over his head, and neither one could stand tall enough to pry it out of his big fat fist. Besides, who the hell would want another Billary administration? Just imagine what trouble Slick Willie could get up to in the White House when he was not amenable to "preserve, protect, and defend the Constitution of the United States." God help us all.

US Congress

22

HOPE & CHANGE

The hagiographical portrayal of Barack Hussein Obama is an amalgamation of genuine celebrity magnetism and the persuasive political appeal of a contemporary demagogue. Along with his good looks, his euphonic name, and cool demeanor, "No Drama Obama" is a refreshing contrast to the archetypical presidential candidate persona, yet one who falls squarely in place as both a radical liberal and a fiscally irresponsible civil servant.

Obama is an African-American in the true sense of the ethnically hyphenated description, but one who does not resemble the standardized version of an average American black male. He is equally white, and he grew up in paradisiacal Hawaii rather than a mainland urban environment. Obama is the product of a bigamous father from Kenya and an eighteen-year-old college student who hailed from Kansas. The couple met at the University of Hawaii in 1960, and within a year they were the married parents of biracial baby Barack.

The following year, Obama's mother ventured to Seattle with her new baby to study and work, leaving her newlywed husband behind. She returned to Hawaii just as her husband departed to Harvard, where he met another woman and quickly abandoned his new family in Hawaii. Obama's mother divorced his father, met and married an Indonesian man, had a baby with him, and moved to Indonesia, leaving Obama behind to be raised by her parents in Hawaii. Hardly a stable home environment for the young Obama, but a compelling saga.

Before returning to Africa with his third wife, the father visited ten-year-old Obama in Hawaii for their last time together. In Kenya, Obama's father struggled with alcohol and poverty and was killed in a car accident, leaving a legacy of four wives and nine children.

As a result of his capricious upbringing, Obama freely admits he was without direction and a constant substance abuser. As a teenager, Obama spent the last two years of his high school career in Hawaii skipping school, drinking beer, doing cocaine, and in a "haze" of marijuana. Obama states in his memoir that he was getting high with both "white" classmates and "brothers." It is now obvious that in spite of his absent African father, Obama considered himself more black than white.

Obama knew very little of the mainland's black urban culture when he arrived in Los Angeles to attend Occidental University in 1979. In his memoir he writes that he carefully selected his friends based on race and his professors on their Marxist teachings, and that he sought out socialist conferences. This is when Obama's adult life becomes murky.

After two years at Occidental, Obama transferred to Columbia University in New York City to complete his college career. Transferring to an Ivy League college midway is an impressive accomplishment for a student with a less than exemplary transcript, which is now sealed. This event has become the provocation of contemporary conspiratorial speculation that Obama was being championed by a sub-rosa consortium within the liberal political illuminati.

After graduating from Columbia, Obama moved to Chicago to become a social activist and community organizer. A few years later, Obama enrolled in Harvard Law School and became the first African-American president of the *Harvard Law Review*. After graduation, Obama returned to Chicago and joined a law firm where he met his future wife, Michelle. Obama also tried his hand teaching constitutional law at the University of Chicago.

This time line also provides hypothetical evidence to conspiratorial fanatics. They believe the systematized matriculation from Columbia to Harvard Law School should have been seamless rather than after a three-year hiatus in Chicago. To support their irrational although accurate thesis, they speculate that Obama relocated from the most populated city on the West Coast to the most populated city on the East Coast to the most populated city in the Midwest and established relationships with radical comrades at every destination.

In Chicago, Obama associated with some rather provocative activists. He served on the board of the Annenberg Challenge Project with domestic terrorist and anarchist Bill Ayers. As a leader of the subversive Weather Underground, Ayers bombed Congress, the New York City Police Department, and the Pentagon. Ayers also co-wrote a book that was dedicated to the convicted assassin of Bobby Kennedy among others.

Obama renounced his Muslim faith to become a Christian and joined the Trinity United Church of Christ. "I am a Christian, and I am a devout Christian. I believe in the redemptive death and resurrection of Jesus Christ. I believe that faith gives me a path to be cleansed of sin and have eternal life."

Obama's pastor for twenty years, Rev. Jeremiah Wright, the man who officiated at his wedding and baptized his daughters, the man whose sermon is the title of Obama's second book, preaches racial hatred rather than Christian acceptance. Furthermore, Wright execrated the United States after the 9/11 attacks, preaching anti-white, anti-Semitic, and anti-American drivel.

Obama also becomes Chicago businessman Tony Rezko's legal representative and later the beneficiary of his political fundraising abilities. Obama later denotes a questionable real estate transaction with Rezko as a "bonehead move." In 2011

Rezko was sentenced to 10 ½ years in federal prison for political influence peddling, receiving kickbacks, and wire fraud. Now that is a foursome in golf.

With the backing of his felonious friends, Obama is elected to the Illinois State Senate in 1996. Eight years later he becomes a candidate for the US Senate and is awarded the coveted opportunity of delivering the keynote speech at the 2004 Democratic National Convention in Boston. This is a rare privilege and justifiably inflames the conspiratorial fanatics. They believe this event confirms that Teddy Kennedy and the political elite were using this opportunity to launch Obama onto the national political stage. They are correct, it did.

During his speech at the convention, Obama announced, "My parents shared not only an improbable love, they shared an abiding faith in the possibilities of this nation. They would give me an African name, Barack, or 'blessed,' believing that in a tolerant America your name is no barrier to success. They imagined me going to the best schools in the land, even though they weren't rich, because in a generous America you don't have to be rich to achieve your potential."

It is interesting why he said such a thing. His father abandoned his "improbable love" and his "blessed" son, returning to Africa with another American wife. He squandered his academic accreditations, funded by wealthy Americans, and died an alcoholic after fathering a litter of children. Additionally, his mother also discarded Obama when she married another man and moved to a foreign land. Obama did attend the best schools in the country, but like his father, he scrapped his Harvard education, paid for by scholarships, and quit the legal profession. Obama won his election for the US Senate and moved to Washington as the freshman senator from Illinois.

Also during this speech, we first heard Obama as the great unifier. He spoke of red states, blue states, and the United States of America. He continued, "Now even as we speak, there are those who are preparing to divide us—the spin masters, the negative ad peddlers who embrace the politics of anything goes. Well, I say to them tonight, there is not a liberal America and a conservative America—there is the United States of America. There is not a Black America and a White America and Latino America and Asian America—there is the United States of America."

All of this got Obama elected in 2008. He is the first African–American to be elected president and he promised a transparent administration of Hope and Change. So far, three and a half years later, it is difficult to find the transparency or the hope or the change. Obama may consider himself to be the great intermediary of ethnic and political divisions, but as president, cultural partitions have never been more polarized.

Slavery came to colonial America as an economic necessity by the British. Most cultures have practiced some version of slavery for millenniums, and the British colonists were no exception. Western African tribal leaders sold their kinfolk to European slave traders, who brought them to America as "indentured servants." After independence from Britain, the United States of America inherited the culture of slavery.

So divisive and profound was the issue of slavery in the formation of the republic that after nearly a century, the South seceded from the Union and civil war broke out. Over a million lives were sacrificed in order to reunite the nation and abolish slavery. One hundred and fifty years ago the nation's population was a mere thirty million citizens, a tenth of what it is today. That is comparable to ten million causalities in 2012. Good did overcome evil, but the Democrats' abolitionist stance on slavery virtually retired them to the sidelines of presidential politics for two score and sixteen years.

The national ambivalence to the mistreatment of blacks since the end of the Civil War, especially in the Deep South, remains historically inexcusable. The federal government has gone to extraordinary lengths to rectify this conduct, but in reality the contemporary behavior of blacks toward other blacks is equally disturbing. Crime remains rampant within the black community.

Statistics released by the Bureau of Justice Statistics reveal that half of all homicide victims in the United States are African-American and 93 percent of these slayings are committed by other blacks. African-Americans are seven times more likely than people of other races to commit murder, and eight times more likely to commit robbery. Accordingly, the 2008 racial composition of the US prison population was 60.21 percent African-American,[16] while African-Americans represented only 13 percent of the general population.

There are forty million blacks in the United States. They enjoy greater freedom and financial prosperity here than any other location on the globe, yet as a minority group, they continue to complain of racial bigotry, even with Obama sitting in the Oval Office.

Taxpayers have contributed trillions of dollars to the entitlement programs of the Great Society, advanced the quota system under the auspices of affirmative action, and summoned Ivy League recruiters waving promises of free college tuition into black communities. Still the black community thinks the government should do more. How much more can be done without assistance from their own community?

Obama claimed during the 2008 election process, "I believe we can provide jobs to the jobless, homes to the homeless, and reclaim young people in cities across America from violence and despair."

Since Obama became president, ethnic unemployment has surged to record levels, home ownership has plummeted, and violence permeates the inner city. According to the *CBS Evening News*, in Chicago, the president's homebase, the homicide rate

---

16 The Bureau of Justice Statistics, US Department of Justice, 2008.

increased by 37.8 percent in the first six months of the 2012. Sgt. Matt Little of Chicago's Gang Enforcement Unit, referred to the crime wave as "tribal warfare". I say go ahead, start doing something and live up to your campaign promises.

Obama has failed many with thoughtless and bigoted comments on delicate social matters. Less than two months into office, Obama self-deprecatingly referred to his inability to bowl as "like Special Olympics or something." Great, the hope and change president who was going to repair divisive commentary just insulted over fourteen million citizens born with intellectual and physical disabilities. It is also fair to point out that it was the sister of Teddy Kennedy, Obama's biggest supporter, who founded Special Olympics, and now Obama is demeaning her life's work and the lives of people with intellectual disabilities with a cheap pejorative joke at their expense on the *Tonight Show with Jay Leno*. Not very appreciative to the Kennedys, and not very presidential.

That summer, when Harvard professor Skip Gates was arrested at his Cambridge home for disorderly conduct, the new president commented, "The Cambridge police acted stupidly" and implied racial profiling. As it turned out, one of the two cops who had been called to the area regarding a housebreak was white and the other was black. When the white cop asked Skip to produce identification, Skip flipped out and accused the white cop of bigotry and insulted the white cop's mother with a phrase one would expect from comedian Eddie Murphy, rather than a highly educated and esteemed member of the Harvard faculty. As it also turns out, Skip did not own the house; Harvard did, so asking for identification was appropriate police protocol. It was only after Skip was outside the house, in handcuffs, that he saw the black cop and realized how badly he screwed up. The president called a "beer summit" with the white cop and Skip to make amends in the Rose Garden. Cambridge dropped the charges, but the stain remained.

The perception is that our newly hired chief executive was more comfortable meddling in the pettiness of community affairs than the affairs of state. To personally speculate on lawful and proper police procedure at a local level rather than use this incident to address the overwhelming national issue of race, poverty, and crime not only defines his activist mentality, but it also trivializes his promised presidential leadership of unification. Furthermore, for a Harvard Law School graduate to nationally malign a hardworking white constable as a racial profiler, without all the facts of the case, is either pure ignorance or the repetitive diatribe of minority victimization, neither of which is impressive and smacks of the *One-Dimensional Man* bathos. Either way it was handled poorly. Perhaps this is why Obama quit the legal profession.

As it pertains to the federal legal system, President Obama beefed up the budget of the Justice Department's Civil Rights division by 18 percent and appointed fellow Columbia graduate and African-American Eric Holder as attorney general. Upon assuming office, Holder stated, "Though this nation has proudly thought of itself as an ethnic melting pot, in things racial we have always been and continue to be, in too many ways, essentially a nation of cowards."

Holder's father emigrated from Barbados to New York City so he and his family could realize the American dream. A Caribbean black relocates to racist and cowardly America, and in his family's first generation, his son enrolls at Columbia University for not one, but two degrees. That son is appointed the first black attorney general by the first African-American president, and then denounces his family's host nation as a group of racial cowards. It is difficult to imagine that as a recipient of "tolerant" and "generous" America, Holder could sound so embittered and unappreciative. Never mind the million lives lost during the bloody Civil War, or the brutal treatment of the Freedom Riders. I believe when Kennedy was killed in Dallas, southern schoolchildren applauded, calling him a "nigger lover," but to Holder, these idealists are cowards.

One issue that has historically plagued American blacks is the voting system. Jim Crow laws allowed local voting stations to administer literacy tests, poll taxes, loopholes, and trick questions that prevented many blacks from voting. The Voting Rights Act of 1965 ended the unequal access for blacks to voting booths, but not whites. When evidence surfaced of an armed group of menacing New Black Panthers members blocking and threatening whites at a voting booth in Philadelphia during the 2008 election, Holder refused to prosecute. When ACORN, the minority voter registration group, one of Obama's pet organizations, was accused of felony voter fraud with plenty of hard evidence to support the charges, Holder refused to prosecute. When a white actor visited Eric Holder's precinct voting booth, he identified himself as "Eric Holder" and was given a ballot. If the actor had used the ballot, I bet Holder would have prosecuted.

"This Department of Justice does not enforce the law in a race-conscious way," stated Holder.

As a result, and because of allegations of continued nation-wide voter fraud, thirty states passed laws that require some form of identification in order to vote. In the case of Indiana, the law was upheld in the United States Supreme Court. Holder's Justice Department rejected South Carolina's 2011 law of voter identification as disproportionately placing an undue burden on minorities, and refers to it as a poll tax. The female minority governor who signed that bill offered transportation to any citizen seeking an identification card, and fifty-three out of five million voters took her up on the offer. If one requires identification to drive a car, enter an office building, or board an airplane, why is proof to vote a burden?

I believe the attorney general should have explained the Justice Department's role in the infamous Fast and Furious "gunwalking" program of giving weapons to Mexican drug lords. Congress sought an explanation, as did the family of a murdered border guard, but again, Holder remained silent. He appeared too busy interfering with states' rights. Holder was found in contempt of Congress for not complying with the

House Oversight and Government Reform Committee for failing to release subpoenaed documents on the subject. As this is a precedent, Obama bailed out his attorney general by throwing the cloak of executive privilege on the matter. Congress called for Holder's disbarment.

Instead of Holder blaming cowards, let this administration utilize the secretary of education and produce some valid institutional structure to keep the seven thousand students who drop out every day in school. Fifty percent of high school students in the nation's fifty largest cities will fail to graduate.[17] Dropouts from the Class of 2010 alone will cost the nation more than $337 billion in lost wages over the course of their lifetimes.[18] If US high schools and colleges were to raise the graduation rates of Hispanic, African-American, and Native American students to the levels of white students by 2020, the potential increase in personal income would add more than $310 billion to the US economy.[19]

If the president wants to do something about hyphenated ethnic designations, he should create a Cabinet position on race relations and repair this division before things become more stretched. The Democrats, and this president in par-

---

17 USA Today, 6/20/2006.

18 Alliance for Excellent Education, "The High Cost of High School Dropouts: What the Nation Pays for Inadequate High Schools" (Washington, DC: Author, October 2007).

19 Demography as Destiny: How America Can Build a Better Future," (Washington, DC: Author, October 2006).

ticular, should be proactive on this point, but that would be confused with leadership.

On the topic of economics, let us look at what Obama inherited from Bush. A year of recession, two very costly foreign wars, rising unemployment, a financial banking disaster, and enormous compounding debt. Obama told us he could get us back on track. "America, our work will not be easy," he said. "The challenges we face require tough choices, and Democrats as well as Republicans will need to cast off the worn-out ideas and politics of the past. For part of what has been lost these past eight years can't just be measured by lost wages or bigger trade deficits. What has also been lost is our sense of common purpose—our sense of higher purpose. And that's what we have to restore."

Just a week after Obama's inauguration, a meteoric trend of increasing unemployment statistics began to rise, hitting the high-water mark of 10 percent in October 2009. The captains of industry knew the economy was going to be in the trenches during the Obama administration, and they protected their bottom line by laying off workers. Historically, the average length of US recessions is thirteen months, but fifty months later the economy continues to sputter, despite what the White House reports.

Although the monthly unemployment rate in mid 2012 is reported at 8.2 percent, in reality the number represents the total amount of unemployment claims filed, not how many people are out of work. At Obama's proclaimed official end of the current recession in June 2009, America was 12.6 million jobs short of full employment. By January 2012, we were 15.2 million unemployed. So much for providing jobs or hope.

When Obama came into office, the nation, and especially the press, expected great domestic accomplishments from a Democratically controlled Washington. Historically speaking, that should have been the case. Wilson was committed to protecting the common man from the heartless industrialists and the power elite; Roosevelt utilized the wealth of the federal government to create jobs for unemployed men, reformed banking practices, and ignited an expansion of home mortgages; Truman tapped Congress to fund anticommunist programs and expand the New Deal; Kennedy promised small business loans and a trip to the moon; Johnson reshuffled entitlement benefits and enacted civil rights; even Carter promised ethics and honesty. Obama promised all that plus transparency, and nothing could be further from the truth.

Obama's greatest miscalculation was forcing the Patient Protection and Affordable Care Act, informally referred to as "Obamacare," through Congress. Speaker of the House Nancy Pelosi stated, "We have to pass the bill so that you can find out what is in it." The Senate's version of the bill is 2,700 pages in length. That is hardly transparent. Furthermore, the bill was not scripted by the Obama administration; it was written by Congress, and he signed it. This is not the progressive congressional cooperation of Wilson or Roosevelt, or any president for that matter. This is partisan bulldozing. A patrician Roosevelt acknowledged and thanked the athwart Republicans for their assistance during his New Deal legislation, but not a word from Obama, and he wonders why he got "shellacked" in the 2010 midterm elections.

Most small business owners do not understand the intricacies of Obamacare or its future economic impact. As a result, they hold steady and refuse to hire employees. The Obama administration now allows "waivers" to special interest groups that do not want or need Obamacare, but if ordinary taxpayers were not to subscribe, they would be fined. The Supreme Court determined that this penalty was in fact a tax, something Obama said it was not. Additionally forty-three Catholic groups have sued the federal government for forcing the mandates of the act on them despite being in direct conflict with Catholic doctrines and theology. This is the works of the "devout" Christian; maybe he should attend church services for inspiration.

Medical insurance is the sixth-largest industry in the country. If the overly educated Obama administration cannot manage to pen the legislation that transitions the health care industry into a bureaucracy, it is inconceivable that the government will ever be able to manage it. Obama's socialist approach to government is unfathomable. The popular evidence is clearly against him. One would not have to look any further than Europe's "cradle to grave" medical care programs for evidence of the economic damage caused by socialized medicine.

The majority of Americans are opposed to Obamacare, but the president believes he knows better. Obama never worked in the private sector; he never created a job, or paid for anything, as far as we know. What is not earned is not appreciated, so when he saddles future generations with the financial obligation of his socialist reform, he is not only denying those kids all the benefits and advantages he received, but he is also burdening them with picking up the tab for his ill-conceived program.

It is important to remember that Wilson offset the missing revenues of foreign tariffs from the budget with income tax revenues. It is one thing to promote progressive legislation; it is another thing to find a way to pay for it. This is exactly what happened to Johnson's Great Society. The taxpayers became fiscally and morally exhausted paying for programs that proved to be futile. This Obamacare initiative is without merit, investigation, or vision; it's just a gamble. I say gamble with your own money or your own health, not mine.

To that point, Obama has not produced a viable budget since coming into office. He stubbornly refuses to compromise with the Republican House leaders and adamantly ignores the recommendations of his personally appointed members of the National Commission on Fiscal Responsibility and Reform to reduce spending and stop accumulating massive debt. For the first time in our history, the United States lost its AAA rating due to the unsustainable $16 trillion debt, most of which is being held by communist China.

Obama continues to blame Bush Jr. for the economic mess the nation finds itself in, and the general voting public has become jaded to his flimsy excuses. If Obama wanted to objectively look back at the economy under Bush Jr., he would find that in post-9/11 America, citizens actually prospered, and it was only after the collapse of the Wall Street derivative market and the bursting of the Democratic Congress's housing bubble in Bush Jr.'s last year of office that the economy tanked.

Obama had a Democratically controlled House and Senate rubber stamp for the first two years of his presidency and failed to resolve our economic troubles. His myopic agenda was Obamacare, and he wasted all of his political currency and congressional goodwill enacting it. As a result, Washington remains hopelessly gridlocked. Without compromise, the government cannot prevent the sunset clauses on tax cuts. This administration's policy wonks and Sunday morning political hatchet men are attempting to blame the Republican House. No one appreciates the blame game in Washington. Losers find excuses, winners find a way. Get a budget and an economic plan together and hammer out leadership legislation. Do something and stop whining.

Even in the wake of Obama's near trillion-dollar stimulus program, the nation is hemorrhaging jobs. Additionally Obama has failed to produce sound mortgage refinancing options for hardworking but now underemployed workers as Roosevelt did. After bailing out the nation's banks and taking over Freddie Mac and Fannie Mae, do you think the Obama White House could get those institutions to relax their lending practices as Roosevelt had done?

Obama expanded Roosevelt's entitlement philosophy by extending unemployment benefits for ninety-nine weeks and enrolling forty-five million people on food stamps. The number of food stamp recipients is up 110 percent in four years, and now more than 5.4 million former workers and families are collecting Social Security disability insurance. Disability ranks have outpaced job growth under President Obama. The Bureau of Labor Statistics reported that in June 2012, the economy added 80,000 jobs, and the Social Security Administration announced that 85,000 workers left the workplace entirely to enroll in the SSDI program the same month. While the economy has created 2.6 million jobs since June 2009, 3.1 million workers have signed up for disability benefits. They are not disabled; they are unemployed and costing the taxpayer billions of dollars. In 2011, disability payments were $130 billion while the trust fund took in only $110 billion. A White House report in late 2011 noted that because "workers on SSDI rarely return to the labor force," this can result "in a loss to society of the economic contribution those workers could have made."

In spite of his extensive education in liberal arts and law, I believe Obama does not understand capitalism and does not feel the need to be better informed. His class-warfare solution is to tax the wealthy. The top 10 percent of wage earners already pay 70 percent of federal taxes, 47 percent of all filers pay no taxes, and 57 percent receive federal benefits. Obama wants the higher income to pay their "fair share", there are less than two workers from every welfare recipient. Who is not paying their fair share? Everyone pays taxes when employed. Let us start there.

Obama's current budget of $3.8 trillion adds an additional $1 trillion to the deficit. That translates into over $9.7 billion federal funds spent each day, which is 50 percent higher than during scapegoated Bush Jr.'s administration. If Obama wants to live up to his promise to reduce the deficit by half at the end of his first term, he better buy a lottery ticket.

President Kennedy cut taxes, the economy expanded and personal savings increased 50 percent. Reagan also cut taxes, and look what happened. After the midterm Republican Congress forced Clinton to cut spending and reduce taxes, the nation enjoyed the greatest economic expansion in our history. Obama the overeducated has proved to be not only fiscally negligent but an economic neophyte who is in way over his head. Maybe he is just a straight-out socialist or champagne liberal hypocrite who preaches, "Do as I say and not as I do."

Obama's personal behavior with federal funds has been fiscally reckless. Obama flies on Air Force One all over the world at record levels and at taxpayers' expense. It costs the American taxpayer $181,000 per hour to fly Air Force One. That means his Hawaiian vacation cost the taxpayer nearly $4 million in air travel alone. He lives in the most beautiful home in America during a time of economic austerity. Do you think he could hang around the White House, shoot up to Camp David for a little golf, and work a little harder to get the country working again? Forget about his wife and her elaborate European vacations, her security details, her aircraft and entourage, or the elaborate parties they throw in the White House. Why can't they not afford a vacation home? Additionally, the White House limousine pool has increased by 73 percent under Obama. Does this make Obama a limousine liberal, or something else?

After JP Morgan's $3 billion quarterly trading loss, Obama beat the table about federal regulation of the financial markets and called on Congress to come up with legislation. Wilson and Roosevelt did not go to Congress with a blank piece of paper in their hands to restructure the financial markets. They appeared with well-researched and highly formulated solutions to the nation's recovery, but they were not in the back pocket of "fat cat bankers on Wall Street," as Obama refers to his contributors.

Following Slick Willie's lead, candidate Obama went to Wall Street and cultivated over $42 million in campaign contributions in 2008, the largest haul from Wall Street to date. As insurance for reelection funds, Obama hired his first two chiefs of staff from Wall Street, the people "who just don't get it." I guess they get running the West Wing. One of Obama's "fat cat" Wall Street bundlers, who later advised him on the economic bailout, is now due for a bailout himself.

John Corzine, former Democratic senator, governor, and Obama bundler, was appointed CEO and chairman of MF Global in March 2010. He resigned in November 2011 after filing the eight-largest bankruptcy in US history. In papers filed in US Bankruptcy Court in Manhattan, MF Global listed debt of $39.7 billion and assets of $41 billion. The loss was determined to be investments in futures contracts and derivatives. A House committee subpoenaed Corzine to respond to questions of the $1.6 billion shortfall in investors' funds. Corzine denied knowledge of the use or misuse of investors' funds to cover company losses. It was determined that the funds were unrecoverable. No word from Holder.

The financial market reform that Obama demanded in 2010 to prevent such abuses fell on the feet of Senator Chris Dodd and Representative Barney Frank. They sponsored the Dodd-Frank Reform and Consumer Protection Act. No one can explain what the act accomplishes or how it is enforced, but it is reform legislation. Furthermore it is ironic that the two biggest perpetrators of the financial meltdown scripted a bill to protect the consumer after skinning them alive.

Obama's position on the nation's dependency on foreign oil consumption and alternative energy sources is equally convoluted.

"Oil and petroleum imports are down an average of more than 1.5 million barrels per day and domestic crude oil production has increased by an average of more than 720,000 barrels per day since 2008. Domestic oil production has gone up every year under President Obama."[20]

Microeconomic theories teach that the greater the supply, the less demand, and prices will fall. If domestic oil production has increased every year under Obama, why then has the price of gasoline doubled during the same period? Is it over-regulation, or pure speculation by his bundlers? Furthermore, here in the United States, the country where Obama wants to reduce foreign oil consumption by a third in the next twelve years, Obama refuses to approve the domestic extension of the Keystone Pipeline that would transport Canadian synthetic crude oil to Texas's Gulf Coast. The extension would mean twenty thousand new jobs, but Obama halted it for environmental issues, just as he has deterred offshore drilling as the result of the BP oil rig explosion in 2010.

It is estimated that there is a sixty-year supply of domestic reserves in US oil fields and another ninety years of reserves in natural gas. In addition to this administration's apprehension over offshore oil drilling and drilling in national parks, it is also skittish on the use of hydraulic fracking to uncover pockets of natural gas, because environmentalists are afraid of water contamination. Natural gas prices have plummeted as a result of locating massive amounts of natural gas by fracking. The Environmental Protection Agency's overregulation of this industry is halting job growth and perpetuating our foreign oil dependence, the antithesis of Obama's message.

---

20 www.barackobama.com

Obama's policies on alternative energies continue to be disingenuous. His secretary of energy, Stephen Chu, wants US gasoline prices to be at parity to those in Europe as an incentive to Americans to buy more fuel-efficient automobiles. It should be noted that the federal fleet of sixty thousand automobiles burns nearly a million gallons of gasoline a day.[21] In 2011, the federal government purchased 2,645 hybrid and electric cars and trucks, or 5 percent of its new fleet, a 59 percent decrease from 2010.

Obama's ideas of "green energy" do not end there. Outside of leaving an enormous carbon footprint with his endless world travel and the huge increase in the White House limousine pool, he still believes that the future lies in alternative energy. "It's a strategy that will keep reducing our dependence on foreign oil, put more people to work, and ultimately stop the spikes in gas prices we've put up with year after year," he said on ABC news. To prove this, his Department of Energy oversaw the outlay of over $16 billion of the 2009 stimulus funds to be used as guaranteed loans to twenty-six solar companies that could not raise funds in the open market. In some cases the executives liquidated their stock positions after federal funding so that they could preserve their financial gains. Obama rationalized his massive lending practices: "Decisions about how Recovery Act dollars are spent will be based on merits, they will not be made as a way of doing favors for lobbyists."

---

21 Government Accountability Office, March 2011.

That policy apparently did not apply to political contributors. Approximately 80 percent of those loans went to campaign contributors of Obama,[22] including former Vice President Al Gore, whose electric car company, Fisker Automotive, received $529 million from the DOE to build cars in Finland[23]. I guess we do not need any more automotive jobs here in the United States and we should use taxpayers' funds to outsource jobs to Finland.

If you were a member of Obama's National Finance Committee, for every dollar you raised, you would receive nearly $25,000 in loans, mostly for green energy start-ups or bailouts. That translates into $457,843 raised and $11.3 billion lent, mostly to current or former employees of Goldman Sachs.[24] The most celebrated case in mainstream media is the $573 million Department of Energy loan to Solyndra, a solar power company that never turned a profit, declared bankruptcy, fired workers, and closed its factory. And with no hope of recouping any of our losses. When the Small Business Administration loaned guaranteed federal funds, there was a litany of requirements that had to be satisfied before the funds were guaranteed, especially having personal capital in the game. Not anymore, and this is not small business—this is a $16 billion disaster. I wonder how many minority plumbers were on that job?

22 Peter Schweizer, Throw Them All Out, Boston, New York: Houghton Mifflin Co., 2011, p. 79.
23 *Ibid.* p. 100.
24 *Ibid.* p. 89

If Obama wants to emulate Europe, he should halt his efforts to develop alternative energy sources. Europe gave up on the concept years ago, citing the enormous expense and poor end result. Obama's Department of Energy appears to approve of projects that cost millions and fail to produce. Obama's green energy "czar," a West Wing employee who sidestepped congressional approval, was social activist Van Jones, a self-proclaimed radical and avowed communist. Is it necessary to mention how much time and money Roosevelt, Truman, and Eisenhower spent to contain communists? Shall we determine how many American lives were lost during the Asian conflicts and the Cold War? Don't forget about Kennedy. He was assassinated by a communist, and now Obama has a radical anarchist who is a student of Marx and Lenin working in the White House? This does not sound like my father's Democratic Party. Thank goodness for Glenn Beck's unrelenting persecution of Jones' employment in the White House, as it resulted in getting the commie czar fired.

This is a pretty sad state of domestic affairs for Obama and the Democrats. Race, crime, a weak economy, high unemployment, rising gas prices, and horrific lending practices. On the international front, things do not seem any better.

During the election of 2008, Obama promised two things: to end Bush Jr.'s wars on terror and to close the Guantanamo Bay detention camp, referring to "Gitmo" as a "sad chapter in American history." He has accomplished neither since being elected.

During the interregnum, Obama and his nascent administration were made privy to the president's daily security brief-
ings. Just as Kennedy had learned, the global situation truly was
as bad as he asserted during the campaign. In Obama's case,
they were worse. The gathering of intelligence has become a
full-time occupation for the West Wing. There are domestic
concerns, and then there is only the rest of the world. Our true
enemies are terrorists without borders, generals, or diplomats,
and they are constantly trying to kill us.

There is also the concern of fighting two foreign wars
in two separate but seemingly notorious hostile nations. No
one has ever succeeded in Afghanistan; Alexander the Great,
Genghis Khan, the British, and recently the Russians attempted
to invade what is now Afghanistan, but the nationals would
not hear of it. Over a million Afghans died fighting Russian
forces before the Russians finally retreated in disgust. A civil
war followed, and the religious extremist Taliban took control
when the sand settled. There are many religious extremists in
the Middle East, and none is happy unless someone from the
opposing religious extreme group is being brutally killed in
God's name.

Bush liberated Iraq because Saddam Hussein would not
agree to UN inspections for nuclear weapons, or weapons of
mass destruction, and Iraq had been a general pain in the ass
for far too long. It was naive to think that the Middle East was
any place but a hotbed of catastrophic consequences. Failure
in Iraq was not an option.

Obama had no prior experience with the military, and now he was commander in chief. He may have ideologically removed the word "terror" from the reality of our military conflicts, but that does not remove the reality that international terrorists are trying to kill Americans and develop offensive nuclear weapons.

Obama pragmatically determined it would be best to keep Bush's secretary of defense on board until he found his footing. Secretary Robert Gates stuck around for 2½ years until Obama could find a replacement. Once again, Obama was in way over his head, but now it was foreign policy. Obama approved and deployed a recommended military surge that he opposed as a senator during Bush Jr.'s term. My, how things change.

Without merit, Obama was awarded the Noble Peace Prize. It is implausible for a recipient to be granted this peaceful accolade for increasing military presence in Iraq and Afghanistan. After awarding the same distinction to Al Gore for a fable documentary on global warming, it appears that the liberal illuminati have infiltrated the Parliament of Norway, and the once globally respected award has now been rendered meaningless.

The reason that international terrorists remain incarcerated at Guantanamo Bay is because Obama now knows there is no better place to keep them and no better place for the United States to conduct proceedings against them. Obama signed an executive order to that effect, and Congress agreed. Obama has given up trying to prosecute the terrorists in United States courtrooms, and even Holder finally concurred.

When court proceedings began, the terrorists disparagingly laughed at our judicial system and mocked the proceedings by throwing paper airplanes around the courtroom and winking at the horrified families of those killed by the terrorist hijackers on 9/11. Good thing Obama did not bring the extremists stateside. I don't believe he could contain the citizens of the tri-state area, the ones who suffered the greatest personal loss, from storming the bastille.

Additionally, during the campaign, Obama was morally opposed to the use of "enhanced interrogation" by the US government. He called it torture and vowed to end its practice. Now as commander in chief, instead of capturing and politely asking inquiries of the enemy, Obama personally maintains a highly illegal and highly immoral "hit list" of individuals he wants killed. As to not suffer any unnecessary casualties, the commander in chief deploys unmanned drones into sovereign airspace to adroitly annihilate his targets.

By killing the terrorists, rather than capturing them, Obama denies his own intelligence agencies the opportunity to extract information from the combatants. In one case, Obama ordered the killing of an American-born terrorist in a foreign land. That is the political assassination of a treasonous US citizen by the president of the United States and the execution of a citizen without due process under United States military or criminal law. Our constitutional law professor president, marvelous. Holder said nothing.

It was the details extracted during enhanced interrogation sessions that were pieced together, over an onerous period of time, which finally located the most wanted man in the world, our archnemesis: Osama bin Laden. After ten years of battle, we had him in our sights, and Obama gave the kill order. There was no black-ops plan to kidnap or contain bin Laden. It was a kill order, but who could blame us? The new president acted very Bush Sr. and demurred from any boastful celebration, as to not inflame a tinderbox of emotional and religious reaction in the Middle East.

On the one-year anniversary of the killing of bin Laden, Obama took a fourteen-thousand-mile victory lap to visit the troops in Afghanistan and beamed a campaign speech back to the United States to revel in "his" successful endeavor. How much did that political trip cost the taxpayers, and why are national military issues being used as campaign balderdash?

Immediately there was an official Obama campaign advertisement featuring Bill Clinton of all people. The guy who let bin Laden escape prior to the terrorist attacks mused, "The downside would have been horrible for (Obama), and he did take the harder and the more honorable path." Now we know why bin Laden successfully evaded Clinton.

Furthermore, Obama took advantage of the occasion to make political hay, speculating that the Republican nominee for the 2012 election would not have ordered the killing of bin Laden, a military power only Obama possesses. Mitt Romney glibly responded, "Even Jimmy Carter would have killed Osama bin Laden." Joe Biden chimed in to say that "bin Laden is dead and General Motors is alive." GM might still be alive, but it owes the American taxpayer $50 billion.

Hypocrisy has become a virtue in Washington. A Nobel Peace Prize recipient should not be glorifying political assassination. A president who is rapidly withdrawing troops from Iraq and Afghanistan just in time for reelection should not be taunting the enemy. The commander in chief should not be self-aggrandizing himself on global satellite television when it was the previous administration, the one he faults for just about everything, that established the intelligence infrastructure and interrogation tactics that led to location of bin Laden. Obama gave the order, but he did not pull the trigger. The SEALs should get the recognition; a true leader would know that.

What is so disheartening about this administration is that, prior to the inauguration, the nation had so much hope and there was so much promise. The nation elected a prophet, but it fizzled. It was all folly and little policy. Furthermore, Obama's failure at leadership establishes validity to the pessimistic naysayers who have become so distrustful of politicians and have lost all faith in our government, most demonstratively, the Tea Party.

The partisan animosity in Congress and its relationship with this inconsequential presidency charts a trend that defines what the average citizen believes: that Washington cares more about itself than the people it serves, and as a result, we now expect so much less from our politicians—less honesty, less honor, and less character.

As Obama seeks to close down the wars in Iraq and Afghanistan, he also comes up short on other foreign policy matters. Any American can go to Berlin and pound his chest about the United States' successful military actions in Europe, the Berlin Airlift, the Marshall Plan, our commitment to NATO, our support of the EU. But when Obama toured Europe as an international extension of his presidential campaign in the summer of 2008, he never articulated his boastful spirit as a proud American. He was really only seeking campaign footage. It was not until after Obama was in office that we learned he was fundamentally embarrassed by previous US foreign policy. Funny he never brought up that fact until he was elected. The man is a fraud.

When Obama returned to Europe as president, he apologized to our allies for our "failure" to accept Europe's role in world politics, and said that he regrets US foreign policy for exhibiting "arrogance" and for being "dismissive." Are you kidding me? There are over 125,000 US military personnel buried in Europe because the Europeans could not get along with their neighbors. That is not our fault; we saved their asses, twice. Obama should watch the first twenty minutes of *Saving Private Ryan* and keep his conciliatory mouth shut. When de Gaulle withdrew from NATO and requested that President Johnson remove all US troops from French soil, Johnson wondered out loud if that included the bodies of the sixty thousand interned servicemen who died liberating France.

Obama also apologized to Muslims for "mistakes" and to the world for "darker periods" of United States history. I do not know what mistakes were made with Muslims, but I am acutely aware that he was apologizing for the segregation of blacks in the south and the "crack of the whip" on the backs of slaves. No Kenyans ever endured segregation or the crack of a whip in the United States. Maybe he should be apologizing to the wealthy American families who elevated his father's academic standing, only to have him throw it all away. Maybe Obama should apologize to the taxpayers of Massachusetts for hosting and housing his aunt and illegal drunk-driving uncle, but please do not apologize to the world on my behalf. During slavery in the United States, my ancestors were being starved by the British.

Recently when US soldiers in Afghanistan burned a Koran that set off a violent protest, Obama apologized with alacrity. "I wish to express my deep regret for the reported incident...I extend to you and the Afghan people my sincere apologies." As a matter of interest, the Koran was burned because it contained hidden codes the military could not decipher. There was no reason to apologize. We were defending freedom and democracy in Afghanistan, and it was costing US soldiers' lives. John McCain would not have apologized, and I don't believe Roosevelt, Truman, or Kennedy would have either. Clinton, I dare not speculate; there is nothing he would not do.

In March 2012 an open microphone disclosed a hushed dialogue between Obama and Russian President Dmitry Medvedev. Obama covertly asked him to convey a message to incoming president Vladimir Putin, a former KGB spy, that when Obama gets reelected, he will have more latitude to lessen US missile defense programs. Apparently Obama does not realize that Russia has already shared our antimissile defense research with North Korea, Red China, and Iran. I am sure that every commander in chief since Truman is turning over in his grave at the thought of such a feeble foreign policy approach to the Russians. The mainstream media still mocks conspiratorial theorists who believe that Obama is a "Manchurian president," but it is not just the "birthers" or the conspiratorial fanatics who believe it.

As far as Iran is concerned, what is our policy? It is the epicenter of global terrorism and has been our greatest international foe since 1979. I appreciate that the economic sanctions are working with respect to selling Iranian oil in the global market, but what does Obama say to Benjamin Netanyahu that allows the Israeli prime minister to sleep at night? Is it that we will never negotiate with terrorists and will never allow Iran to produce nuclear weapons? We already sponsored a nuclear-facility attack on Iran by Israel in 1977. Is Obama guaranteeing that to Netanyahu?

What does Obama say to the Iranian protestors who scream "Obama: Are you with us or against us?" as they protest on the thirtieth anniversary of the US Embassy takeover in Tehran? Furthermore, what was our policy in Libya? Hawks say we led from behind, doves believe that Obama violated the War Powers Act, but we have not heard anything about Libya in a while.

What is our stance on Syria? In June 2012 the brutal tyrant Assad killed 108 of his own people; nearly half were women and children. The United Nations protests, but the Obama White House is silent. Just like President Johnson, he critics are coming from the left and the right trying to force him off a menacing cliff. Obama is too busy attacking Mitt Romney and free enterprise while trying to get reelected. Meanwhile the Arab Spring becomes the Arab Winter. All of this reminds me of Clinton, who would say and do anything to get reelected. There is no action or reaction, not even an explanation. And Mailer said Eisenhower was devoid of color.

23

THE IDENTITY CRISIS

The United States is generationally suffering from an iden-tify crisis that is a direct result of the turmoil and tumult in the past two decades. I understand that at different points in time, and for quite different reasons, the United States has touched lower historical troughs, but what we are experiencing now is the abandonment of the core principles of American ingenu-ity. Americans accomplish things in a unique manner that sets us apart from the rest of the world. What is wrong with America is not the conduct of Americans, but the direction that our leaders are taking us. We are dumbing ourselves down in order to assimilate with the general consensus of foreign nations rather than leading by example.

The United States is the ideal the world admires. I have never heard of foreigners trying to sneak into the Soviet Union, or North Korea, only attempting to escape. I never heard of anyone illegally entering Mexico for a job opportunity or to improve their standard of living. I have never heard of anyone going to China to have an anchor baby, and probably never will.

Infanticide is a state sponsored forced abortion for mother's attempting to deliver "excess babies".

We are Americans, and we are different from the rest of the world. We look different, we dress differently, and our manners are distinctively our own. We invented pretty much everything that influences the world today. From electricity, to lightbulbs, to television. From nuclear power, from air travel to space travel. We advaned scientific breakthroughs in medicine and in health care. We have fought foreign wars, not for boundaries, but for world peace. We achieved these things because we believed the objectives were attainable through perspiration, perseverance, and persistence. We distanced ourselves from others who thought them impossible; we should not apologize for our successes—we should celebrate them.

Kennedy sent us to the moon, not just to outpace the Soviets, but also to challenge the heavens and for the national prestige. "We choose to go to the moon in this decade and do the other things, not because they are easy, but because they are hard," he said. We dared to dream and realize our dreams; we are winners, not whiners.

In my opinion, the national press is partially to blame. I thought when the circulation of daily newspapers began to decline, the television media would fill the void. I was wrong. Now, to my amazement, television newscasters interview other journalists for their interpretation of the news, rather than the newsmakers themselves. Is this news? I don't think so. I think it's editorial opinion. I expect a television journalist to explain the facts of the news to me, and I'll make up my own mind. Americans did not like Carter preaching to us or Clinton altering the facts. Why would I want an imbalanced interpretation of the news?

For this reason, cable news has been eating the lunch of network television, and some cable news programs are eating the lunch of other cable new shows. But the world is turning so fast now, it is difficult to keep pace.

What network television requires, and finds unattainable, is a venerable standard bearer, someone like Walter Cronkite, who at one time was considered the most trusted man in America. It is difficult to trust these cable network journalists. They just seem so predictable and disingenuous. News anchors change constantly because of poor ratings and slanted journalism; just look at Dan Rather's fall from grace. Next, with round-the-clock, around-the-world, up-to-the-minute news reporting, programs need a constant stream of drama. News shows do not appear to care about Mrs. O'Leary; they care about why her cow kicked over the lantern that started the fire.

The fact that network news programs have taken the low road in current political drama has reinforced the notion by many that these programs are dominated by a liberal media agenda, and there is sound evidence to support their claim. Although cable television has purged itself of some of the wackiest anchors, there remains some antagonistic reporters who still spew rivers of liberal rhetoric at their guests, inter-rupt those with whom they do not agree, and shake their heads in disagreement, waiting for their opponent to stop talking before they start shouting. To whom is this virulence appeal-ing? It doesn't work in domestic differences or effectively in the workplace, why would any viewer want to listen to individu-als scream at one another? They don't, they change the chan-nel to Fox News.

One cable newscaster who reported that he had "a thrill go up his leg" listening to Obama in 2008 has since denounced the president's administration as aimless and not worthy of a second term. Then Obama goes to Afghanistan for a political victory lap for the death of bin Laden, and the same anchor applauds him and is "proud" of him for acting like a com-mander in chief, which is part of his job description. Now when anyone asks him about his palpable comment, he attacks them as right-wringers. So what is it? Do you like Obama or not? Are you are flip flopper? Please elucidate me. Why not just report the news without all the personal grandiloquence? I cannot believe the same anchor never gave Bush Jr. a break.

In second quarter 2012, MSNBC ratings dropped dou-ble-digits; CNN followed with its lowest ratings in twenty one years. The two networks combined cannot match Fox News' ratings. I am quite sure that the prime time program slot on the East Coast is tuned in to Fox News, with the pos-sible exception of Manhattan and the People's Republic of Cambridge.

By the way, what exactly is a "Democratic strategist"? Do Republicans have them? I see them on different talk shows, but I don't know anything about them. Where did they all come from? I've been around for a while. Am I one? If not, how do I become one? Is there an address I can send my résumé? Where do they work, what degree do they possess, what successful campaign have they managed? I don't know the answer, and no one will tell you. I heard one guest explain how he was a communications director for a political campaign, and then he began discussing foreign affairs. I thought those two topics were separate planes of expertise, and I expected the producer to know that as well.

These Democratic strategists are the ones who say the most offensive and provocative things about Republican candidates, their spouses, and other elected national leaders, and they do it with smirks on their face. Even the president and his spokespeople do it. It is maddening and indicative of how they view their audience and opposing viewpoints overall. Seldom do they stay on topic or answer the questions asked. They go on the defensive and push the extremes farther apart. I thought the definition of an intellectual was one who possessed the ability to understand, to reason by investigation and contemplation, and not to be intolerant. How can one claim to be intellectual when unwilling to debate, discuss, or compromise?

A well-known White House lobbyist—remember no lobbyists in the Obama White House—insulted the wife of the yet-to-be official Republican nominee with the comment that she

"Never worked a day in her life." Ann Romney is the devoted mother to five boys who happens to be married to a wealthy man; she can afford to be a stay-at-home mom. This lobbyist who now claims to be a Democratic strategist is separated from her gay lover and their adopted children. Why is she sniping a woman like Ann Romney? Are her own umbrages seeded in her personal attacks? Ann Romney is not running for president, her husband is, and please do not use the designation of my affiliated party to demean straight women and cancer survivors who are stay-at-home mothers in happy marriages. I am a Democrat, but you do not speak for me. You speak for a far-left liberal subset of my father's Democratic Party, and you crashed my party. Show some respect.

When Rush Limbaugh says something regrettable and calls a congressionally interviewed Georgetown Law School student a "slut" because she wants birth control from a Catholic university, Obama the great unifier telephones her to apologize for a radio talk show host exercising his First Amendment rights, and his reelection campaign calls the statement an attack on women. What? If the student wants to have birth control, she can go buy it. If you can afford to enroll in Georgetown Law, you can afford to pay for protection. If she is accepting financial aid from the Catholic university, she really can't say anything; she did not have to attend a religious campus to attend law school.

Now when a member of the liberal media, Bill Maher, who contributed a million dollars to Obama's super PAC and who is a political commentator, disparagingly and obscenely refers to a female elected official as a woman's sexual organ, there is not a word from anyone. It is the height of hypocrisy.

I feel as if the Democrats of today are addressing a voting base way beyond me, assuring them that "help is on the way" from the vicious Republicans who will no longer be able to hurt them. This is puerile and patronizing. Stop explaining your positions to me as if I am a ten-year-old and quit being so damn condescending, and I will listen. These strategists even attack the opposing point of view's character with ad hominem attacks. Democrats should not be passing judgment on character; they are a little sparse in that department. When Representative Paul Ryan attempts to bring a budget forward, they attack him personally and portray him pushing old ladies off a cliff. Grow up!

On Sunday morning shows, the anchors each week invite the same members of the press and the same strategists for a topical discussion, and together they argue about the same issue from different angles. "Your guy is a jerk and my guy is the solution." He says, she says. I can't believe they are still taken seriously. Instead of changing anchors, the producers should be changing the format.

This discourse has seeped into the international vernacular. How is it that Paul McCartney of the Beatles spent most of his musical career mocking authority, smoking pot, and being a teen idol and late in life becomes a political pundit? The Queen of England extends a meritless and ostentatious title to

Sir Paul, and he comes to the White House to receive an honor from our president, representing our government, and his lordship makes a derogatory comment about our prior president? "After the last eight years, it's great to have a president who knows what a library is," he said. Has Sir Paul earned a degree from Yale or the Harvard Business School, or is he just a mop top with a fancy little decoration the monarch gave him? Is it the same little pin she gave Elton John or Mick Jagger, or is it like the one Sir Paul's bandmate John Lennon returned to her as a protest to it being a war medal? I wonder what song he preformed for Obama. Was it, "Back in the USSR"? Where is the outrage? I would love to see the response by the Fleet Street journalists if Madonna went to #10 Downing Street and slighted the Queen for preserving a birthright of exploitation and oppression.

Furthermore, what are movie actors and musicians doing insulting the president and his policies when US troops are on the ground? Did they attend the Jane Fonda school of international indignity? I am not interested in an actor's opinion of a war or hearing them slag the commander in chief at a foreign venue. I don't want them to embarrass me or preach to me, I want them to entertain me. Who are these self-righteous individuals who live in a self-indulgent world to pass judgment on elected officials? If they want to do some good, either run for office or give their movie money away to charity. I love seeing billionaire Irish rocker Bono exiting a private transport on an African plain, carrying a $1,600 valise in a luggage advert after complaining about the lack of US funding for the African AIDS epidemic.

Who is this guy Michael Moore, and who is he to perspicaciously judge anyone? If he wants to judge someone, start with Clinton. His administration failed to heed the threats of the jihadists and allowed them to bomb us repeatedly, with impunity, and bring their demented form of fanatical religion and terrorism into the United States and kill three thousand innocent people.

My idea of Democrats are disciplined intellectuals who respect the office of president, no matter who sits in the Oval Office, and do not criticize their commander in chief in a global exercise of personal speculation. Documentaries are slanted portrayals by definition, but to profess that 9/11 was an inside job is insanity. Who would Moore have preferred at the helm, Al Gore? Would that have prevented the attacks? Gore was a complicit coconspirator in the administration that condoned bin Laden, so what exactly is Moore's point?

If Democrats want to do good things, here are two challenges: Do something about continued illegal immigration and do something about skyrocketing entitlement benefits. When the entitlement programs were expanded during the Great Society, there were 18 workers to every welfare recipient-in 2012 there are less than two workers for every recipient.

How Islamic jihadists can come into the Unites States, take flying lessons, get driver's licenses, travel around the country, come and go as they like and not raise red flags is beyond me. I know law-abiding European citizens who are required to show bank balances and pay stubs to immigration officials to visit the United States. How can the southern borders remain open to all those who seek illegal entry into the United States? I don't care about illegal Mexicans coming into my country looking for a free meal or a day's wages; I care about Islamic terrorists illegally entering my country hoping to kill my kids.

I get that Woodrow Wilson came into office not because he was a popular candidate but because Teddy Roosevelt was a spoiler in the general election. I also appreciate that Wilson made amazing progressive legislative achievements, bringing the nation into the industrialized twentieth century, aiding the farmer, keeping the factories safe and the consumer protected, and also getting control of the banking system.

I understand the reason Harding and Coolidge succeeded Wilson. I empathize with the apolitical Herbert Hoover for being out of touch with the nation's economic events and broken spirit, and that an optimistic Roosevelt was required to unseat him. I grasp that Roosevelt's extraordinary legislative and military successes were the reasons that Americans kept him in office for four terms. I agree that the Constitution needed revising as a result of King Franklin's monarchy, and I believe that Harry Truman's arrival in 1945 was divine intervention. I am infinitely impressed with how Truman responded

312

to his Herculean tasks, especially dropping the atomic bomb without regret. I believe he deserved to get reelected, and I'm glad he did.

I know why Ike Eisenhower was elected: to keep us safe and to let the grass grow over the graves of the sixty million casualties of WWII, and to keep pressure on the communists from creating more graveyards. No nation wanted to mess with Eisenhower. For a while he was the leader of the sole superpower, and he had a well-known itchy trigger finger.

I am delighted that Jack Kennedy defeated Dick Nixon in 1960, not just because of the personal contact my family had with his administration, but rather that Nixon was not commander in chief during the diplomatic struggles with the Soviets and the Cubans. Kennedy played chess while Nixon would have been playing checkers, excuse the pun. It would have been catastrophic had Nixon been president. We would just be crawling out of the bomb shelters now, fifty years later.

I also know that Kennedy's assassination was a plot, maybe a solitary coup d'état, but the plot of at least one communist, and it changed the entire direction of the country. I understand that Lyndon Johnson was a better senator than a president and sympathize with his struggles of how and why he got dragged into Vietnam. I believe if Kennedy had lived, we would be a better nation today.

I acknowledge that Nixon's successful presidential campaign in 1968 was because of the combined events of that horrible year. I also know it was his own paranoia and deceitful demeanor that drove him from office. His second vice president, Gerald Ford, took over and kept the floors clean, but he was still a segment of the Watergate scandal. Ford's pardon of Nixon brought about the wishy-washy administration of Jimmy Carter.

I acknowledge that Carter was too Christian and thus politically naive and never should have never been elected, but because he was a weak president, we were able to traverse Watergate and elect Ronald Reagan. I disliked Reagan in his first term, not because he was a Republican, but because he was a Democratic turncoat. I admired him in his second term; he was good for the country.

I gather that George Bush Sr. appeared wimpy because he was a gentlemanly WASP, and I appreciate what he accomplished to carry on Reagan's foreign policy, which led to the end of the Soviet Union and honor in the Persian Gulf. I understand that after twelve years on the nation's tab, it was time for him to retire. But for the life of me, I will never understand why, after we put our collective faith in Bill and Hillary Clinton, they led us down a garden path that will never lead us back to Reagan's shining city on a hill.

How we will get back there will require more than a leader with ambition, more than a politician with vision, but a president who cares more about the common good of the country than about his legacy. "It is amazing what you can accomplish if you do not care who gets the credit," articulated Harry Truman.

George Bush the younger was not that man, although he tried. After the second World Trade Center bombings, he identified the lapses in security and created a new Cabinet position to address it. I know he took a group of young military volunteers to the deserts of Iraq and Afghanistan to wage war against an invisible enemy, but something had to be done. Some are critical that his decisions, blessed by Congress, were based on erroneous intelligence, but I believe he tried his best with the information he had on hand, and I believe it was because of the failed Clinton policies that we were attacked, not because of Bush.

"If Saddam rejects peace and we have to use force, our purpose is clear. We want to seriously diminish the threat posed by Iraq's weapons of mass destruction program." President Clinton commented on February 17, 1998. He knew what was going on in Iraq, but chose to do nothing.

I know Bush's critics are plentiful, egged on by a far-left and liberal press. I know that if Cindy Sheehan had been able to properly educate her son, per John Kerry, he would not have had to reenlist in the Army and die in Iraq. But that is not Bush's fault. Soldiers are expendable. I do not know why she demeans the honor of her son's sacrifice by claiming the war was to make Bush's friends rich from oil. Please do not misjudge me as a fan of George W. Bush; I'm only a supporter of his presidential conduct.

This persecution of Republicans by the press began with Nixon and Watergate. We all know Nixon was corrupt and exposure by the press caused his resignation. We all saw how Ford was mocked for falling down stairs or announcing that the Poles were not under Soviet domination. We all know that Reagan was a septuagenarian who took a few naps during White House meetings. We know that Bush Sr. did not know what a barcode scanner was, but what the press did to Bush Jr. was unholy.

If the press wants to go after the core of the division that exists in this country, start with Clinton. He polarized Congress, and he gave credibility to the accusation that all politicians are corrupt liars and unfaithful to their wives. He sold our soul to Wall Street, and Americans are still paying the price.

As a former president, Harry Truman would not take a corporate position for fear that "You don't want me. You want the office of the president, and that doesn't belong to me. It belongs to the American people, and it's not for sale." When Congress determined that Truman was living penuriously in Missouri, they began the Former Presidents Act, which allowed for a pension and other governmental benefits.

Does it surprise you that Clinton earned $75 million in speaking fees since leaving office, two-thirds of the haul from international venues? Not me. I believe it starts there, in the area of accountability.

If I could think of one reason why members of Congress no longer speak to one another, that the Senate feels no compunction to produce a budget in the past three years and remains unwilling to compromise, to do its job, to enact laws, that citizens no longer trust government, why young girls think oral sex really is not sex, why we were attacked on 9/11, why the economy and the housing market was derailed by Wall Street speculators, it is because of Bill Clinton's exploitation of institutions; there is nothing he and his wife would not do, and they are somehow still doing it. The greatest compliment to my father's Democratic group was, "There's no whore in him." I cannot imagine what they would say about the Clintons.

The IRS reckons that cheating on one's personal income tax returns is three times higher since Clinton was president. The Secret Service has been caught not just hiring prostitutes during foreign advance security sweeps but for not paying them for their services, and Obama, their ultimate boss, tells little jokes about it. Isn't that cute? The GSA has spent millions of taxpayers' dollars on junkets to Las Vegas, and now an ICE official is accused of getting kickbacks. The Department of Justice is selling, check that, arming Mexican drug lords, that killed a federal boarder patrol officer and Obama's national security officials are leaking sensitive information to the press to extol Obama in an election year.

What the hell happened to America? The absence of being a Republican does not make one a Democrat. I remain a Democrat, but I don't know what the hell happened to the party or who some of these people are. They appear to be self-serving, far-left socialists; they are no longer my Democratic leaders.

24

SMALL-BALL POLITICS

So now we head into the election season of 2012. It's been a hundred years since Wilson showed up and changed the Democratic Party into the progressive powerhouse that we know and love, or hate, today. Wilson is the first modern president, yet he hails from a period when there were more horses than humans living in the United States. It's hard to imagine everyday life without automobiles, cellular telephones, or televisions, when adults died of influenzas and children were crippled by polio, before brave Americans headed off to fight world wars in exotic lands, and before man headed out into space and inhabited, for just a few days, that Paleolithic orb, the moon.

Roosevelt had the radio and his fireside chats to reassure Americans. Kennedy had televised press conferences to make his point. Today Obama has the Internet and has used it well to create a massive fund-raising resource and to connect to the younger generation.

Barack Obama has not had an easy job being president these past three and half years, but he wanted the job. In spite of his uncommon circumstance, he has benefited much in life. I admire his pursuit and his conquests, but it is truly time to stop with the social reengineering of the United States and elect a man into office who can get this country back on track and back working again. I wish that man were a Democrat. The late Joe Moakley, the "dean" of the New England Democratic delegation, used to say about himself and Tip O'Neill and guys of their ilk, "We went to Washington to do good things, to help people." I don't think they make guys like that anymore. If they do, they don't run for office.

I wish I could find those guys, the hard hat union workers, the patriotic veterans, the moral equivalent of those who survived the Great Depression, survived war, the guys who went to college on the GI Bill, the guys and now the gals who went to college, got married, earned a living, bought a house, started a family, and had a few drinks with the neighbors listening to baseball on the radio and grilling on the barbecue. I know those nostalgic historic days are gone, and I understand in contemporary America that people do not experience the same social filtering system. There are so many personal challenges. People today are connected to the World Wide Web, and don't know their next door neighbor. I know there was a lot of downside to those nostalgic days, but I can't help but think there exists capable politicians who are altruistic enough not to worry about polls and self-absorbed reelection bids.

So now Americans have a choice for whom to vote. There is the Republican, Mitt Romney, the former head of Bain Capital, who made more than a few investors millionaires, a Mormon who ran the Olympic Games in Utah, and served one term a governor of my home state. Then there is my party's choice: Barack Obama, whose ideology and track record I find wanting.

About four years ago I was invited to a casual dinner party in my hometown of Brookline. Everyone was having a pleasant time, chatting, the television was on for some reason, and a comedian was doing a pretty good imitation of a bumbling George Bush Jr. In walks this large, loud woman, who throws her bag down, shuts off the television set, and begins a monologue of lambasting Bush Jr. and Republicans. Being slightly amused at this cartoonlike character, I began to bait her. She took every lure I threw at her, and she started shouting at me, calling me a Republican fat cat, as if that were the lowest amoeba in the sewage system.

Someone noticed her drowning and tried to rescue her. They explained that I was a Democrat whose father had converted the leafy town of Brookline into a bastion of liberal Democrats. She looked at me in a different light and asked me why I opposed her turning off the television program. I contritely replied, "If you had listened for a minute, you might have appreciated the satirical performance of the skit." "So what's your point?" she asked. I replied, "I don't think you are the ideal those Democrats had in mind when they took on the Republicans sixty years ago. You can't even watch a lampoon

of a Republican without flipping out and shutting off a TV."
It's fair to say that there wasn't much more to talk about. I left
my hometown to the recent interlopers who relocated there
because of its liberal reputation, and headed home.

I feel the same way about the election this year. There is
no civil discourse, there is no understanding, and there is no
listening. The president flies around on Air Force One campaigning about how the Republicans are not leading, while
they remain in Washington working on a budget and he is out
complaining about them. That is not leadership, that is finger-pointing, and when you point your finger, there are three
pointing back at you.

Obama is a great campaigner, an appealing icon for liberal America, but he is incapable of leading. He needs Teddy
Kennedy, and he is not here anymore. There are no refined
ranking members in the Democratic Party otherwise; Obama
would know better than issuing insensitive remarks from the
White House concerning opponent's wives, their political contributors, or questioning their nationalism. For that matter, it
was the quisling wife of Obama who campaigned that she was
not proud of America, in spite of her Ivy League education and
her high paying job.

Furthermore, Obama's team hacked into the biographical
sketches of former presidents on the White House website and
enhanced the highlights of Obama's first term as compared
with his predecessor's accomplishments. This is a government

website, not a political portal. As one might think that spray-can graffiti is urban art, to the owner of the building it is vandalism. This behavior is vandalism.

The president's Democratic contemporaries, Massachusetts Governor Deval Patrick and Newark Mayor Corey Booker, both African-American, are attempting to bring some civility to the rhetoric by defending Mitt Romney's "sterling" record at Bain Capital and the deploring the nauseating campaign tactics aimed at him. Bill Clinton is trying to support Obama, but it is nearly impossible with the reckless comments the president broadcasts about the economy. It is as if Obama is running a campaign against capitalism when he attacks Romney. If one were to look at Obama's website, it is all about Romney's weaknesses and not about Obama's strengths or record. If Obama wants to omit the word *terror* out of our military jargon, then he should exclude the expression Republican "reign of terror" from of his political discourse.

The wars are not over, Gitmo is not closed, and the enemy combatants have not been brought to the United States for trial. The economy continues to slide back into a recession, if we ever were out of the last one. Race relations remain deplorable. Just look at the handling of the Trayvon Martin case. Eric Holder refuses to admit there is more to the story on Fast and Furious, and dodges the truth at congressional hearings. Next Holder appoints two special prosecutors to determine what member of the White House Security Council leaked national security data to the *New York Times.*

What does Obama have to say about his White House security leaks, which appall even fellow Democrats? "The notion that my White House would purposely release classified national security information is offensive." Does he not read the *New York Times*? The reporter on the story citied of member of his security team as his source. Did Obama miss the articles? Did his press secretary? Usually presidents try to prevent security leaks from landing in the press, but this reporter acknowledges he was given sensitive details on Obama's hit list, the DNA testing of bin Laden by a doctor now in jail, and cyberattacks on Iran nuclear facilities. And by the way, whose White House is it? Ours or his? This is a small-ball attitude to very grave issues. Again, politically contrived and morally maddening.

The president has no record to run a campaign on. I do not hate the guy. I just do not think he has the solution to our national emergency of compounding debt. I believe he is a stubborn academic who is in way over his head and who is unwilling to listen and learn. The best and the brightest of his staff have left. Simpson Bowles was ignored. It's not working, it's time for the country to move on.

Obama keeps talking about finding jobs. They are not hidden in a White House closet; they are created by business owners to help improve the bottom line. The private sector creates jobs and wealth, and the public sector pays salaries and benefits. No one, except senators and representatives, get rich working for the government. If Obama had attended the Harvard Business School instead of the law school, he would know that.

You can say Romney is a venture capitalist. He is. But please do not call him a vampire or a vulture, because he is not. Imagine if Romney called Obama a witch doctor. Furthermore, it is highly Pecksniffian for Obama to lambast Romney for his successful track record in private equity and proceed to ask private equity executives for political contributions. That hypocrisy resonates.

The Founding Father's drafted the Constitution to make all men equal. The Progressives leveled the economic playing field for workers, the New Deal improved people's lives and proud veterans created the middle class. That middle class is now vanishing, and union membership has been halved. The Federal Reserve reports that the median net worth of families plunged 39 percent in just three years, from $126,400 in 2007 to $77,300 in 2010. That puts American families approximately at parity with where they were in 1992.

The Progressives sought to eliminate the patronage of Boss Tweed's Tammany Hall. Conversely, Obama has been funding wealthy campaign contributors' speculation, especially in solar power, is redolent of cronyism and ultimately denies the middle class a chance to succeed; this is the fundamental antithesis of Roosevelt's Democratic Party. Kennedy's small business owners, who hire workers, are the hidden closets where jobs truly exist. That is where Obama's attention should be— not Hollywood, not Wall Street, but Main Street. Money was meant to be earned, not given away. What is not earned is not appreciated.

If Obama wants to debate capitalism and claims that Romney and Bain Capital actually lost jobs, good luck. Romney secured profits for willing investors. Obama, on the other hand, invested unwilling and unknowing taxpayers' funds into Solyndra and lost $500 million. BP contributed $71,000 to Obama's campaign, and he returned the favor with a $308 million loan that created twenty-thee jobs. Furthermore, the Obama administration lent Al Gore over $500 million to build cars in Finland. If Romney shared Obama's investment track record, he would be serving fries at a fast-food restaurant.

How do you think Romney got so wealthy? Because he earned it. The federal debt continues to grow, and interest compounds at astronomical levels. Forty cents on every dollar is borrowed. Meanwhile, Obama and his Sunday morning-show surrogates claiming that the administration is creating new private sector jobs is a canard.

In July 2012, Obama stated, "If you've got a business, you didn't build that. Somebody else made that happen." This statement validates my point precisely; he does not understand economics or the entrepreneurial spirit. My mother told me many times of my father sleeping in his warehouse to ensure urgent medical deliveries were properly expedited in the morning. These are the sacrifices small business owners make. There are family members, employees and vendors depending on them. What is not earned is not appreciated.

I would like to know a little bit more about Obama's stance on gay marriage. In Illinois, he was for it. As a presidential candidate, he was against it, and now he is for it again. Although the subject remains extremely provocative in most cultures, it is not here in Massachusetts. When no one was really paying attention, a judge ruled that it was unconstitutional under the Massachusetts constitution to allow only heterosexual couples to marry. Governor Mitt Romney responded by approving town clerks to commence issuing marriage licenses to same-sex couples. First in the nation—that is a position.

The edict caught on like wildfire in the Northeast and Iowa. Other states began to allow same-sex marriages. Some states took a more conventional route and proposed legislation or put the initiative on state ballots, and the propositions failed, especially in California of all places. In my opinion, the United States government and the Obama administration has bigger fish to fry than worrying about gay marriage. The Defense of Marriage Act, passed by both Houses of Congress and signed by Bill Clinton, federally defines marriage as a legal union between one man and one woman.

In reality, same-sex marriage is not just about couples loving each other and raising children. It is more about civil rights and shared benefits. What the government should not be doing is politicizing the topic during a reelection cycle. Vice President Joe Biden makes his personal, not official, position to support gay marriage known to the press one day, and the next day apologizes to Obama for bringing the controversial subject public during the campaign. The White House issues an official statement and reaffirms the president's opposition to gay marriage. Two days later candidate Obama capitulates and now supports gay marriage and immediately attacks Mitt Romney for opposing it and his reelection website begins to market pro-gay-rights apparel!

If Obama wants to support gay marriage, script legislation to change the Defense of Marriage Act. This is small-ball amateur hour for the Democrats.

All of this proves that Obama is a trendy Wendy with his finger in the air waiting for the direction of the wind to set him on course. It failed for Kerry on the windsurfing board; it is foolish to emulate flip-flopping on any subject, especially one so controversial.

In 1960 the press asked Kennedy if he was exhausted campaigning against Nixon so vigorously. Kennedy rejected the idea, stating that it was Nixon who should be tired, for every time Nixon speaks he needs to know how to address that specific crowd, and that would be exhausting. But Kennedy just showed up and spoke his mind; to be yourself is not exhausting. That is the policy Obama should be using, but then again, we do not know whom Obama really is.

Obama's new support of same sex marriages backfired. It was obviously manufactured to drum up support in the most liberal of communities, which is the analogous to addressing "ethnics" in an ethnic dialect, which is equivalent to racism. In spite of the majority of African-Americans' opposition to same-sex marriage, the NAACP came out and backed the gay marriage initiative in support of Obama. What I would prefer is for the NAACP to come out in support of heterosexual marriage, as 72.3 percent of African-American children are born out of wedlock, and 38 percent are born into poverty.

This was the same week that African-American Desmond Hatchett of Tennessee admitted to fathering over thirty children with eleven different women in the past fourteen years. "I had four kids in the same year. Twice," he said. Under law, when Hatchett is working, he is required to turn over 50 percent of his minimum wage salary for child support. Some of the mothers of Hatchett's children get only $1.49 a month. Guess who picks up the balance? You do.

If Obama wants to include the cost of abortions to be picked up by the American taxpayer, I am all for it. Just send Desmond Hatchett's girlfriends to the clinics first. I can't afford to support any more children than my own.

EPILOGUE

So back here in Massachusetts we are having a power drain of political clout. The once-proud epicenter of New England Democratic liberalism is declining. Due to a population shift, we lost a congressional seat. Our controversial congressman Barney Frank is retiring, as congressional redistricting would put him at a blue-collar disadvantage and also because, "I don't even have to pretend to try to be nice to the people I don't like." This rationale is from our recently married, openly gay congressman who demands tolerance. Good riddance. Our congressional delegation no longer produces speakers of the house or congressional deans; we retain career politicians who never seem to accomplish much, except to be reelected.

One would think that after the embarrassment of the Democrats not being able to hold on to Teddy Kennedy's Senate seat, they would come up with a better candidate to challenge Scott Brown in the 2012 election.

Elizabeth Warren is an extended version of Martha Coakley. Only this woman is a minority Harvard Law School professor. Formerly, she was a bankruptcy attorney who worked with Senate Majority Leader Harry Reid during the 2008 TARP bail-out, and with Obama in the creation of the controversial United

States Consumer Financial Protection Bureau, a byproduct of the Dodd-Frank Act, which Obama dishonestly staffed with a recess appointment, even though the Senate was in session.

Similar to Hillary Clinton, Elizabeth Warren was a Republican who converted to the Democratic Party. She has impressive liberal qualifications and has been on all the liberal media shows, including the miscreant misogynist Bill Maher's, and in Michael Moore's film: *Capitalism: A Love Story.* Her defenders include the lesbian lobbyist who attacked Ann Romney and the anti illegal immigrant-tracking Governor Deval Patrick, another one of David Axelrod's clients.

Warren also supports the Occupy Wall Street protestors, claiming, "I created much of the intellectual foundation for what they do." The National Republican Senatorial Committee immediately criticized her support. "Warren's decision to not only embrace, but take credit for this movement is notable considering the Boston Police Department was recently forced to arrest at least 141 of her Occupy acolytes in Boston the other day after they threatened to tie up traffic downtown and refused to abide by their protest permit limits."[25]

Warren also claimed to be Native American and was Harvard's first minority hiring of such. She later explained that she checked off the Native American designation so that other Harvard Native Americans might invite her to lunch. No one called, so in order to tempt her fellow tribesmen, she contrib-

---

25 NRSC spokesman Brian Walsh wrote to the Boston Globe, 10/25/2011.

uted recipes to a Native American cookbook, *Pow Wow Chow.* Warren claims she is 1/32 Cherokee and that her grandfather had high cheekbones, "Like all the Indians do." Just slightly racist from the blonde and blue-eyed academic.

So in the absence of Teddy Kennedy, we met Republican Scott Brown, a regular guy with a pickup truck and a military uniform. In contrast, the best the Democrats can do is nominate Elizabeth Warren, the warrior princess of the Reid, Obama, Dodd, and Frank alliance. For whom do you think I shall cast my vote for as my US senator?

Made in the USA
Lexington, KY
28 August 2012